CROCHI

Gifts From the Heart™

General Information

Many of the products used in this pattern book can be purchased from local craft, fabric and variety stores, or from the Annie's Attic Needlecraft Catalog *(see Customer Service information on page 63)*.

Introduction

A thoughtful gift, made by hand and given from the heart, is always the very best kind of present. With that in mind, *Gifts From the Heart* offers a delightful collection of gift ideas to please anyone who appreciates being remembered on special occasions, or to brighten the lives of others who are less fortunate.

The enticing projects in *Gifts From the Heart* include great designs for everyone. You'll find adorable designs for babies and kids, cozy comforts for seniors, warm accessories for the entire family (including pets!), snuggly afghans and decorative home accents. All of these special gifts are sure to be appreciated by friends and family as well as charitable organizations that assist our neighbors in need.

Cozy accessories such as hats and scarves, slippers and socks, mittens and wraps are everyday staples of warm winter wear. This delightful array of patterns in a variety of designs and sizes for the family are sure to please even the most discerning tastes in style.

Mother-Daughter Hats & Mittens

Designs by Sheila Leslie

FINISHED SIZES

Toddler's Hat: 17–18 inches in diameter
Girl's Hat: 19–20 inches in diameter
Woman's Hat: 21–22 inches in diameter

MATERIALS

☐ Red Heart Soft Baby light (sport) weight yarn (7 oz/575 yds/198g per skein):
Toddler's:
  1 skein #7001 white
☐ Red Heart Super Saver medium (worsted) weight yarn (8 oz/425yds/226g per skein):
Girl's:
  1 skein #579 plum
☐ Bernat Illusions bulky (chunky) weight yarn (5 oz/195 yds/140g per skein):
Woman's:
  2 skeins #27959 lilac hues
☐ Size H/8/5mm crochet hook or size needed to obtain gauge
☐ Tapestry needle
☐ Safety pins or other small markers

GAUGE

Toddler's: 9 sc = 2 inches
Girl's: 4 sc = 1 inch
Woman's: 3 sc = 1 inch

SPECIAL STITCHES

Shell: (2 dc, ch 1, 2 dc) in indicated st or sp.
Beginning shell (beg shell): (Ch 3, dc, ch 1, 2 dc) in indicated st or sp.

INSTRUCTIONS
HAT
All Sizes
Note: *Do not join rnds unless otherwise specified. Mark first st of each rnd with safety pin or other small marker.*

Rnd 1: Beg at top of Hat, ch 2, 6 sc in 2nd ch from hook. *(6 sc)*
Rnd 2: 2 sc in each sc around. *(12 sc)*
Rnd 3: [Sc in next sc, 2 sc in next sc] around. *(18 sc)*

Rnd 4: [Sc in each of next 2 sc, 2 sc in next sc] around. *(24 sc)*
Rnd 5: [Sc in each of next 3 sc, 2 sc in next sc] around. *(30 sc)*
Rnd 6: [Sc in each of next 4 sc, 2 sc in next sc] around. *(36 sc)*
Rnd 7: [Sc in each of next 5 sc, 2 sc in next sc] around. *(42 sc)*
Rnd 8: [Sc in each of next 6 sc, 2 sc in next sc] around. *(48 sc)*
Rnd 9: [Sc in each of next 7 sc, 2 sc in next sc] around. *(54 sc)*
Rnd 10: [Sc in each of next 8 sc, 2 sc in next sc] around. *(60 sc)*
Rnd 11: Sc in each sc around.
Rnd 12: [Sc in each of next 5 sc, 2 sc in next sc] around. *(70 sc)*
Rnds 13–16: Rep rnd 11. At end of rnd 16, join with sl st in beg sc.
Rnd 17: Beg shell *(see Special Stitches)*, in same st as joining, sk 2 sc, sc in next sc, sk next sc, [**shell** *(see Special Stitches)* in next sc, sk 2 sc, sc in next sc, sk next sc] around, join with sl st in 3rd ch of beg ch-3. *(14 shells)*
Rnd 18: Sl st in next dc, (sl st, beg shell) in shell sp, sc in next sc, [shell in next shell sp, sc in next sc] around, join with sl st in 3rd ch of beg ch-3.
Rnds 19–21: Rep rnd 18.
Rnd 22: Sl st in next dc, (sl st, beg shell) in shell sp, dc in next sc, [shell in next shell sp, dc in next sc] around, join with sl st in 3rd ch of beg ch-3.
Rnd 23: Ch 1, sc in same st as joining, sc in each dc around, join with sl st in beg sc. *(70 sc)*
Rnds 24 & 25: Ch 1, sc in same sc as joining, sc in each rem sc around, join with sl st in beg sc.
Rnd 26: Ch 1, [sl st in next sc, ch 1] around, join with sl st in beg sl st. Fasten off.

TODDLER'S & GIRL'S MITTENS
Make 2.
Cuff
Rnd 1: Ch 24, join with sl st to form ring, ch 3 *(counts as first dc through-*

out), dc in each rem ch around, join with sl st in 3rd ch of beg ch-3. *(24 dc, counting beg ch-3 as first dc)*
Rnd 2: Ch 3, **fpdc** *(see Stitch Guide)* around post of next dc, [dc in next dc, fpdc around post of next dc] around, dc in same st as beg ch-3, join with sl st in 3rd ch of beg ch-3. *(25 sts)*
Rnd 3: Beg shell in same st as joining, sk 2 sts, sc in next st, sk next st, [shell in next st, sk 2 sts, sc in next st, sk next st] around, join with sl st in 3rd ch of beg ch-3. *(5 shells)*
Rnds 4–6: Rep rnd 18 of Hat. At end of rnd 6, fasten off.

Hand
Note: *Do not join rnds unless otherwise specified. Mark first st of each rnd with safety pin or other small marker.*
Rnd 1: Join yarn with sl st in first rem lp of foundation ch at base of rnd 1 of Cuff, ch 1, sc in same st as joining; sc in each rem lp around, join with sl st in beg sc. *(24 sc)*
Rnd 2: [2 sc in next sc] twice, sc in each of next 22 sc, join with sl st in beg sc. *(26 sc)*
Rnd 3: Sc in next sc, 2 sc in each of next 2 sc, sc in each of next 11 sc, 2 sc in each of next 2 sc, sc in each of next 10 sc. *(30 sc)*
Rnd 4: 2 sc in each of next 2 sc, sc in next sc, 2 sc in each of next 2 sc, sc in each of next 25 sc. *(34 sc)*
Rnd 5: Sc in each sc around.
Rnd 6: Sc in next sc, ch 3, sk 7 sc for thumb opening, sc in each of next 26 sc.
Rnd 7: Sc in each sc and each ch around. *(30 sc)*
Rnds 8–10: Rep rnd 5.
Rnd 11: Sc in each sc around, working **sc dec** *(see Stitch Guide)* in 2 sts over center of thumb opening and sc dec in 2 sts halfway around at opposite *(little finger)* side. *(28 sts)*
Rnd 12: Sc in each st around.

There is new strength, comfort and inspiration in fresh apparel.

—*Ella Wheeler Wilcox*

Rnds 13–16: Rep rnds 11 and 12 alternately. *(24 sts at end of rnd 16)*
Rnd 17: [Sc in each of next 6 sc, sc dec in next 2 sts] around. *(21 sts)*
Rnd 18: Rep rnd 12.
Rnd 19: [Sc in next sc, sc dec in next 2 sc] around. *(14 sts)*
Rnd 20: Rep rnd 12.
Rnd 21: [Sc dec in next 2 sc] around. *(7 sts)*
Rnd 22: [Sc dec in next 2 sts] 3 times, sl st in last st. Leaving a short length for finishing, fasten off. With tapestry needle, weave length left for finishing through sts of last rnd, pull to close opening. Fasten off.

Thumb

Note: *Do not join rnds unless otherwise specified. Mark first st of each rnd with safety pin or other small marker.*
Rnd 1: Join yarn with sl st in first sk st of rnd 5, ch 1, sc in same st as joining, sc in each of next 6 sc, sc over end st of rnd 6, sc in rem lp of each of next 3 chs. *(11 sc)*
Rnds 2 & 3: Sc in each sc around.
Rnd 4: Sc in each of next 4 sc, sc dec in next 2 sc, sc in each of next 5 sc. *(10 sts)*
Rnds 5 & 6: Rep rnds 2 and 3.
Rnd 7: [Sc dec in next 2 sc] 5 times, join with sl st in beg sc dec. Leaving a short length for finishing, fasten off.
With tapestry needle, weave length left for finishing through sts of last rnd, pull to close opening. Fasten off.

WOMAN'S MITTENS
Make 2.
Cuff

Rnds 1–6: Rep rnds 1–6 of Cuff for Toddler's and Girl's Mittens.

Hand

Rnds 1–3: Rep rnds 1–3 of Hand for Toddler's and Girl's Mittens. *(30 sc at end of rnd 3)*
Rnd 4: 2 sc in each of next 2 sc, sc in next sc, 2 sc in each of next 2 sc, sc in each of next 12 sc, 2 sc in each of next 2 sc, sc in each of next 11 sc. *(36 sc)*
Rnd 5: Sc in each sc around.
Rnd 6: Sc in next sc, ch 4, sk next 7 sc for thumb opening, sc in each of next 28 sc.
Rnd 7: Sc in each sc and each ch around. *(33 sc)*
Rnds 8–10: Rep rnd 5.
Rnd 11: Rep rnd 11 of Hand for Toddler's and Girl's Mittens. *(31 sts)*
Rnd 12: Rep rnd 12 of Hand for Toddler's and Girl's Mittens.
Rnds 13–22: Rep rnds 11 and 12 alternately. *(21 sts at end of rnd 22)*
Rnd 23: Rep rnd 19 of Hand for Toddler's and Girl's Mittens.
Rnd 24: [Sc dec in next 2 sts] around. *(7 sts)*

Rnd 25: [Sc dec in next 2 sts] around, sl st in last st. Leaving a short length for finishing, fasten off.
With tapestry needle, weave length left for finishing through sts of last rnd, pull to close opening. Fasten off.

Thumb

Note: *Do not join rnds unless otherwise specified. Mark first st of each rnd with safty pin or other small marker.*
Rnd 1: Join yarn with sl st in first skipped sc of rnd 5, ch 1, sc in same st as joining, sc in each of next 6 sc, sc over end st of rnd 6, sc in rem lp of each of next 4 chs, sc over next end st of rnd 6. *(13 sc)*
Rnds 2 & 3: Sc in each sc around.
Rnd 4: Sc in each of next 5 sc, sc dec in next 2 sc, sc in each of next 6 sc. *(12 sts)*
Rnd 5: Sc in each st around.
Rnd 6: [Sc in each of next 4 sc, sc dec in next 2 sc] around. *(10 sts)*
Rnds 7 & 8: Rep rnd 5.
Rnd 9: [Sc dec in next 2 sc] around, join with sl st in beg sc dec. Leaving a short length for finishing, fasten off.
With tapestry needle, weave length left for finishing through sts of last rnd, pull to close opening. Fasten off. ❏❏

North Country Caps

Designs by Michele Wilcox

SKILL LEVEL

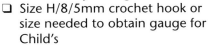

BEGINNER

FINISHED SIZES
Adult's: Brim: 22 inches unstretched
Child's: Brim: 21 inches unstretched

MATERIALS
- Medium (worsted) weight yarn: **4 MEDIUM**
  - Child's
  - 5 oz/250 yds/142g MC
  - 1 oz/50 yds/28g CC
- Bulky (chunky) weight yarn: **5 BULKY**
  - Adult's
  - 6 oz/210 yds/171g MC
  - 2 oz/70 yds/56g CC
- Size H/8/5mm crochet hook or size needed to obtain gauge for Child's
- Size J/10/6mm crochet hook or size needed to obtain gauge for Adult's
- Yarn needle
- 5-inch-square cardboard piece

GAUGE
Size H hook and medium (worsted) weight yarn: 9 sc = 2 inches
Size J hook and bulky (chunky) weight yarn: 7 sc = 2 inches

PATTERN NOTE
To change color in single crochet, work last single crochet before color change as follows: insert hook in indicated stitch, yarn over with working color, draw up a loop, drop working color to wrong side, yarn over with next color, complete single crochet.

INSTRUCTIONS
HAT
Brim
Row 1: With MC for Child's Cap and

CC for Adult's, ch 13, sc in 2nd ch from hook, sc in each rem ch across, turn. *(12 sc)*

Row 2: Ch 1; working in **back lps** *(see Stitch Guide)* only, sc in each sc across, turn.

Rows 3–75: Rep row 2. At end of row 75, do not turn. Do not fasten off.

Cap
Row 1(RS): Ch 1; working across long edge, sc over end st of each row across, changing to MC in last

sc for Adult's. Fasten off CC. For both Caps, turn. *(75 sc)*

Rows 2–4: Ch 1, sc in each sc across, turn.

Row 5: Ch, 1, sc in each sc across, working [**sc dec** *(see Stitch Guide)* in next 2 sc] 3 times evenly sp across. *(72 sts)*

Rows 6 & 7: Ch 1, sc in each st across, turn.

Row 8: Ch 1, sc in each sc across, working [sc dec in next 2 sc] 6 times evenly sp across. *(66 sts)*

Rows 9–13: Rep row 6.
Row 14: Rep row 8. *(60 sts)*
Rows 15–17: Rep row 6.
Row 18: Rep row 8. *(54 sts)*
Rows 19–22: Rep row 6.
Row 23: Rep row 8. *(48 sts)*
Rows 24–26: Rep rows 15–17.
Row 27: Rep row 8. *(42 sts)*
Rows 28-30: Rep rows 15–17.
Row 31: Rep row 8. *(36 sts)*
Rows 32–36: Rep row 8.
Row 37: Rep row 8. *(30 sts)*
Rows 38–41: Rep rows 19–22.

Row 42: Rep row 8. *(24 sts)*
Rows 43–47: Rep row 6.
Row 48: Rep row 8. *(18 sts)*
Rows 49–55: Rep row 6.
Row 56: Rep row 8. *(12 sts)*
Rows 57–66: Rep row 6.
Row 67: Rep row 8. Fasten off. *(6 sts)*

Finishing
With matching yarn and yarn needle, sew Brim and Cap seam. Fold Brim upward onto Cap.

Tassel
Wrap CC around cardboard piece to desired thickness. Cut 12-inch length of CC and pass under yarn at top of cardboard piece. Tie ends securely tog and knot. Cup yarn at bottom of cardboard piece apart. Remove cardboard. Cut 2nd 12-inch length of CC and tie approximately 1½ inches from top of Tassel. Trim ends evenly. Attach Tassel to center of row 67 at top of Cap. ❏❏

Slipper Boots

Design by Elsie Caddey

SKILL LEVEL
INTERMEDIATE

FINISHED SIZES
Instructions are for up to 8-inch sole *(small)*. Changes for 9-inch sole *(medium)* and 10-inch sole *(large)* are in [ ]. When only 1 number is given, it applies to all sizes.

MATERIALS
- ❏ Red Heart Classic medium (worsted) weight yarn (3½ oz/99g/190 yds per skein): 2 skeins dark sage #633 (A) **[4 MEDIUM]**
- ❏ Red Heart TLC Essentials medium (worsted) weight yarn (6 oz/326 yds/170g per skein): 1 skein each celery #2615 (B) and persimmon #2254 (C)
- ❏ Sizes F/5/3/75mm and H/8/5mm crochet hooks or size needed to obtain gauge Tapestry needle

GAUGE
With size F hook and 2 stands held tog: 15 sc = 4 inches
With size F hook and 1 strand: 9 sc = 2 inches
With size H hook and 1 strand: 4 sc = 1 inch

PATTERN NOTE
To change color in single crochet, work last single crochet before color change as follows: insert hook in indicated stitch, yarn over with working color, draw up a loop, drop working color to wrong side, yarn over with next color, complete single crochet.

SPECIAL STITCH
Split single crochet (split sc): Insert hook through center of sc and under top 3 bars and between back strands *(see illustration)*, yo, draw up lp, complete sc.

INSTRUCTIONS
SLIPPER
Make 2.
Sole
Row 1: With size F hook and 2 strands A held tog, beg at Heel, ch 4, 2 sc in 2nd ch from hook, sc in next ch, 2 sc in last ch, turn. *(5 sc)*
Row 2: Ch 1, 2 sc in first sc, sc in each sc across to last sc, 2 sc in last sc, turn. *(7 sc)*
Rows 3–14: Ch 1, sc in each sc across, turn.
Row 15: Rep row 2. *(9 sc)*

Sizes Medium & Large Only
Rows 16–18: Rep row 3.
Rows 19–22 [26]: Rep rows 15–18 consecutively. *(11 [13] sc at end of row 22[26])*

All Sizes
Rows 16–25 [23–27, 27–32]: Rep row 3.
Row 26 [28, 33]: Ch 1, sk first sc, sc in each sc across to last 2 sc, **sc dec** *(see Stitch Guide)* in last 2 sc, turn. *(7 [9, 11] sts)*
Rows 27–28 [29–32, 34–37]: Rep rows 16 [23, 27] and 26 [28, 33] alternately. *(5 [5, 7] sts at end of row 28 [32, 37])*
Row 29 [33, 38]: Ch 1, sk first st, sc in each st across to last st, ch 1, sl st in last st. Fasten off. *(3 [3, 5] sc)*

Heel
First Side
Note: Heel and Toe will be worked around entire Sole into end sts of rows along sides or into bottoms and tops of sts across Heel and Toe ends of Sole.
Row 1: With size H hook, working in rem lps of foundation ch on row 1 of Sole, join 1 strand A with sl st in rem lp at base of center sc of row 1, ch 11, sc in 2nd ch from hook, sc in each of next 9 chs, sl st in next 2 sts or row ends on Sole, turn. *(10 sc)*

Row 2 (RS): Ch 1; working in **back lps** *(see Stitch Guide)* only, sk sl sts, sc in each sc across, turn.

Row 3: Ch 1; working in back lps only, sc in each sc across, sl st into each of next 2 row ends or sts on Sole, turn.

Rows 4–12 [16, 22]: Rep rows 2 and 3 alternately. At end of row 12 [16, 22], turn, do not fasten off.

Toe

Note: *Continue to work all rows of Toe in back lps only unless otherwise specified.*

Row 1: Sl st in each of first 2 sc, 2 sc in next sc, sc in each rem sc across, sl st over end st of each of next 2 row ends or sts on Sole, turn.

Row 2: Ch 1, sk last 2 sl sts made, sc in each across to first sl st, sl st in each sl st, turn. *(11 sts)*

Row 3: Ch 1, sl st in each sl st across to first sc, sl st in each of first 2 sc, 2 sc in next sc, sc in each rem sc across, sl st over end st of each of next 2 row ends or sts on Sole, turn.

Rows 4–8: Rep rows 2 and 3 alternately, ending with a row 2. *(14 sts at end of row 8)*

Row 9: Ch 1, sl st in each sl st across to first sc, sl st in each of next 2 sc, 2 sc in next sc, sc in each sc across to last sc, 2 sc in last sc, sl st over end st of each of next 2 row ends or sts on Sole, turn.

Row 10: Ch 1, sk 2 sl sts, sc in each rem sc, sl st in each rem sl st across, turn. *(16 sts)*

Rows 11 & 12: Rep rows 9 and 10. *(18 sts at end of row 12)*

Row 13: Ch 1, sl st in each sl st across to first sc, sl st in first sc, 2 sc in next sc, sc in each sc across to last sc, 2 sc in last sc, sl st over end st of each of next 2 row ends or sts on Sole, turn.

Rows 14 & 15: Rep rows 12 and 13. *(22 sts at end of row 15, not counting last 2 sl sts worked into edge of Sole)*

Row 16: Sk 2 sl sts, hdc in each of next 5 sc, sc in each rem sc and sl st in each rem sl st across, turn.

Row 17: Ch 1, sl st in each sl st across to first sc, sl st in first sc, 2 sc in next sc, sc in each st across to last hdc, 2 sc in last hdc, sl st over end st of each of next 2 row ends or sts on Sole, turn. *(24 sts, not counting last 2 sl sts worked into edge of Sole)*

Row 18: Rep row 16.

Rows 19–22: Rep rows 17 and 18 alternately. *(28 sts at end of row 22)*

Row 23: Ch 1, sl st in each sl st across

to last sl st before first sc, sc dec in last sl st and first sc, sc in each rem st across to last 2 sts, sc dec in last 2 sts, sl st in each of next 2 row ends or sts on Sole, turn.

Row 24: Ch 1, sk 2 sl sts, sc in each sc and sc dec, sl st in each sl st across, turn. *(26 sts)*

Rows 25–28: Rep rows 23 and 24 alternately. *(22 sts at end of row 28)*

Row 29: Ch 1, sl st in each sl st across to 2 sl sts before first sc, sc dec in next 2 sl sts, sc in each rem st across to last 2 sts, sc dec in last 2 sts, sl st in each of next 2 row ends or sts on sole, turn.

Row 30: Rep row 24. *(20 sts)*

Rows 31–40: Rep rows 29 and 30 alternately. At end of row 40, turn. Do not fasten off. *(10 sts at end of row 40)*

Heel
2nd Side

Row 1: Working across last row of Toe, rep row 3 of Heel First Side.

Rows 2–12 [16, 22]: Rep rows 2 and 3 of Heel First Side alternately, ending with row 2 and last sl st in same st as joining sl st on Heel First Side. At end of row 12 [16,22], do not fasten off. Remove hook from lp. With separate strand of A and tapestry needle, sew first and last rows tog for center back seam.

Top

Rnd 1: With RS facing, using size F hook, pick up dropped lp; working over ends sts of rows around, sk first row of Heel First Side, [sc in next row, sk next row] 2 [5, 10] times, sc in each of next 7 [5, 1] rows, work 15 sc evenly spaced across next 40 rows of Toe section; working across Heel Second Side, sc in each of next 8 [6, 2] rows, [sk next row, sc in next row] 2 [5, 10] times. Do not join. *(34 [36, 38] sc)*

Rnd 2: Ch 1, [**split sc** *(see Special Stitch)* in next sc, changing to B; split sc in next sc, changing to A] around, join with sl st in beg split sc.

Rnd 3: Ch 1, split sc in same split sc as joining, changing to C; split sc in next split sc, changing to A, [split sc in next split sc, changing to C; split sc in next split sc, changing to A] around, join with sl st in beg split sc. Fasten off C.

Rnd 4: Ch 1, split sc in same split sc as joining, changing to B; split sc in next split sc, changing to A; [split sc in next split sc changing to B; split sc in next split sc, changing to A] around, join with sl st in beg split sc. Fasten off B.

Cuff

Row 1: Ch 23, sc in 2nd ch from hook, sc in each rem ch across, sl st in each of next 2 sts on rnd 4 of Top, turn. *(22 sc)*

Row 2: Ch 1, sk sl sts, sc in back lp only of each sc across, turn.

Row 3: Ch 1, sc in back lp only of each sc across, sl st in each of next 2 sts on rnd 4 of Top, turn.

Rows 4–34 [36, 38]: Rep rows 2 and 3 alternately around, ending with row 2 and working last sl st in same st as joining sl st. At end of row 34 [36, 38], fasten off, leaving short length for finishing.

With A and tapestry needle, sew first and last rows tog for center back seam. ❑❑

Designs by Ruthie Marks

SKILL LEVEL

INTERMEDIATE

MAN'S HAT & SCARF
FINISHED SIZES

Scarf: 7 inches wide x 62½ inches long not including fringe
Hat: Fits head 21½ inches in diameter

MATERIALS

- ❑ Medium (worsted) weight wool yarn (4 oz/200 yds/100g per skein):
    2 skeins #240 beige *(A)*
    1 skein each #1405 medium brown *(B)* and #1444 dark brown *(C)*
- ❑ Sizes H/8/5mm and J/10/6mm crochet hooks or size needed to obtain gauge
- ❑ Tapestry needle

GAUGE

Size H hook: 13 sc = 4 inches
Size J hook: 11 sc = 4 inches

INSTRUCTIONS

SCARF
First Half

Row 1: With size H hook and A, ch 24, sc in 2nd ch from hook, sc in each rem ch across, turn. *(23 sc)*

Row 2: Ch 3 *(counts as first dc throughout)*, dc in each sc across, turn.

Row 3: Ch 1, sc in each dc across, turn.

Row 4: Ch 3, dc in each of next 5 sc, dc in **front lp** *(see Stitch Guide)* only of next sc, dc in each of next 9 sc, dc in front lp only of next sc, dc in each of last 6 sc, turn

Row 5: Ch 1, sc in each of first 4 dc, sc in **back lp** only *(see Stitch Guide)* only of next dc, sc in each of next 3 dc, sc in back lp only of next dc, sc in each of next 5 dc, sc in back lp only of next dc, sc in each of next 3 dc, sc in back lp only of next dc, sc in each of next 4 dc, do not turn. Fasten off.

Row 6 (RS): Join B with a sl st in first sc, ch 1, sc in same sc, sc in each of next 3 sc, *dc in rem lp of next dc in row before last, **fpdc** *(see Stitch Guide)* around post of next dc in row before last, tr in rem lp of next st in 3rd row below, fpdc around post of next dc in row before last, dc in rem lp of next dc in row before last, sk 5 sc on last row directly behind last 5 sts worked*, sc in each of next 5 sc, rep from * to *, sc in each of last 4 sc, turn.

Row 7: Ch 3, dc in each of next 5 sts, dc in front lp only of next st, dc in each of next 9 sts, dc in front lp only of next st, dc in each of last 6 sts, turn.

Row 8: Rep row 5.

Rows 9 & 10: With C, rep rows 6 and 7.

Row 11: Rep row 5.

Row 12: With A, rep row 6.

Rows 13–69: Rep rows 2–12 consecutively, ending with a row 3. At end of row 3, do not fasten off. Turn.

Row 70: Ch 3, dc in each dc across, turn.

Row 71: Ch 1, sc in each dc across. Fasten off.

2nd Half

Rows 1–71: Rep rows 1–71 of First Half. At end of row 71, fasten off, leaving length for finishing.

With tapestry needle and length left for finishing, sew last rows of First and 2nd Halves tog through back lps.

Loop Fringe

Cut 100-inch strand of each color.

Row 1: With size H hook, RS facing, join B with sl st in first rem lp of foundation ch at base of row 1 on either Half; working in rem lps across, [ch 12, sk 2 sts, sl st in next st] across, leaving last st unworked. Fasten off. Do not turn. *(7 ch-12 lps)*

Row 2: Working behind ch-12 lps of row 1 with size H hook, join A with a sl st in next unworked rem lp of foundation ch at beg of row, ch 12; working in front of next ch-12 lp, sl st in next unworked st of foundation ch, [ch 12, remove hook from lp, bring ch and working yarn through center of same ch-12 lp to back, pick up dropped lp; working in front on next ch-12 lp, sl st in next unworked st on foundation ch] across, ending with sl st in last st. Fasten off. Do not turn. *(7 ch-12 lps)*

Row 3: Working behind first ch-12 lp of last row with size H hook, join C with a sl st in next unworked rem lp of foundation ch at beg of row, ch 12; working in front of next ch-12 lp of last row, sl st in next unworked st of foundation ch, [ch 12, remove hook from lp, bring ch and working yarn through center of same ch-12 lp of last row and ch-12 lp of row before last to back; working in front of lps, sl st in next unworked st of foundation ch] across to last unworked st of foundation ch. Fasten off.

Rep across rem short edge on other Half of Scarf.

HAT

Row 1: With size J hook and A, ch 60, sc in 2nd ch from hook, sc in each rem ch across, turn. *(59 sc)*

Row 2: Ch 3 (counts as first dc throughout), dc in each of next 3 sc, dc in front lp only of next sc, [dc in each of next 9 sc, dc in front lp only of next sc] across to last 4 sc, dc in each of last 4 sc, turn.

Row 3: Ch 1, sc in each of first 2 dc, sc in back lp only of next dc, sc in each of next 3 dc, sc in back lp only of next dc, [sc in each of next 5 dc, sc in back lp only of next dc, sc in each of next 3 dc, sc in back lp only of next dc] across to last 2 dc, sc in each of last 2 dc. Do not turn. Fasten off.

Row 4 (RS): With size J hook, join B with sl st in first sc, ch 1, sc in same sc, sc in next sc, *dc in rem lp of next dc in row before last, fpdc around post of next dc in row before last, tr in rem lp of next st in 3rd row below, fpdc around post of next dc in row before last, dc in rem lp of next dc in row before last, sk 5 sc on last row directly behind last 5 sts worked**, sc in each of next 5 sc, rep from * across to last 2 sc, ending last rep at **, sc in each of last 2 sc, turn.

Rows 5 & 6: Rep rows 2 and 3.

Row 7: With C, rep row 4.

Rows 8 & 9: Rep rows 2 and 3.

Row 10: With A, rep row 4.

Row 11: Ch 3, dc in each st across, turn.

Row 12: Ch 3, sc in each dc across, turn.

Row 13: Ch 1, sc in each of first 9 sc, [sc dec (see Stitch Guide) in each of next 2 sc, sc in each of next 8 sc] across, turn. (54 sts)

Rows 14–16: Ch 1, sc in each st across, turn.

Row 17: Ch 1, sc in each of first 7 sc, sc dec in next 2 sc, [sc in each of next 7 sc, sc dec in next 2 sc] across, turn. (48 sts)

Rows 18 & 19: Rep row 14. At end of row 19, fasten off. Turn.

Row 20: With size J hook, join B with sl st in first sc, ch 1, sc in same sc, sc in each rem sc across, turn.

Rows 21 & 22: Rep row 14.

Row 23: Ch 1, sc dec in first 2 sc, [sc dec in next 2 sc] across, turn. (24 sts)

Row 24: Rep row 14.

Row 25: Rep row 23. Leaving long length for finishing, fasten off.

Loop Fringe
Cut 60-inch strand of each color.

Row 1: With size J hook, RS facing, join B with sl st in first st of last row, [ch 12, sk 2 sts, sl st in next st] across to last 2 sts, leave last 2 sts unworked. Fasten off.

Row 2: Working behind ch-12 lps of row 1 with size J hook, join A with a sl st in next unworked st at beg of row, ch 12; working in front of next ch-12 lp, sl st in next unworked st, [ch 12, remove hook from lp, bring ch and working yarn through center of same ch-12 lp to back, pick up dropped lp; working in front on next ch-12 lp, sl st in next unworked st] across to last st, leave last st unworked. Fasten off. Do not turn. (7 ch-12 lps)

Row 3: Working behind first ch-12 lp of last row with size J hook, join C with a sl st in next unworked st at beg of row, ch 12; working in front of next ch-12 lp of last row, sl st in next unworked st, [ch 12, remove hook from lp, bring ch and working yarn through center of same ch-12 lp of last row and ch-12 lp of row before last to back; working in front of lps, sl st in next unworked st] across to last unworked st of foundation ch. Fasten off.

Finishing
With tapestry needle, using colors to match sections worked, sew ends of rows tog. With length left for finishing on last row, weave length through sts of last row, pull tightly to gather.

Edging
With RS facing, using size J hook, join A with sl st in first rem lp of foundation ch at base of row 1 of Hat; working in rem lps around, ch 1, [sl st in next st, ch 1] around, join with sl st in beg sl st. Fasten off.

The sense of being well-dressed gives a feeling of inward tranquility.

—C.F. Forbes

WOMAN'S HAT & SCARF
FINISHED SIZES
Scarf: 7 inches wide x 62½ inches long not including fringe
Hat: Fits head 19½ inches in diameter

MATERIALS
❑ Plymouth Encore Classic medium (worsted) weight yarn (4 oz/200 yds/100g per skein):
  2 skeins #1231 dark sage (A)
  1 skein each #1232 medium sage (B) and #1233 light sage (C)
❑ Size H/8/5mm and size I/9/5.5mm crochet hook or sizes needed to obtain gauge
❑ Tapestry needle

GAUGE
Size H hook: 13 sc = 4 inches
Size I hook: 3 sc = 4 inches

INSTRUCTIONS
SCARF
First Half
Rows 1–71: Rep rows 1–71 of Man's Scarf First Half.

2nd Half
Rows 1–71: Rep rows 1–71 of Man's Scarf First Half.

Loop Fringe
With size H hook, RS facing, join A with sl st in first rem lp of foundation ch at base of row 1 on either Half; [ch 24, sl st in next st] across. Fasten off.
Rep across rem short edge on other Half of Scarf.

HAT
Row 1: With size H hook and A, ch 60, sc in 2nd ch from hook, sc in each rem ch across, turn. (59 sc)
Row 2: Ch 3 (counts as first dc throughout), dc in each of next 3 sc, dc in

front lp only of next sc, [dc in each of next 9 sc, dc in front lp only of next sc] across to last 4 sc, dc in each of last 4 sc, turn.

Row 3: Ch 1, sc in each of first 2 dc, sc in back lp only of next dc, sc in each of next 3 dc, sc in back lp only of next dc, [sc in each of next 5 dc, sc in back lp only of next dc, sc in each of next 3 dc, sc in back lp only of next dc] across to last 2 dc, sc in each of last 2 dc. Do not turn. Fasten off.

Row 4 (RS): With size H hook, join B with sl st in first sc, ch 1, sc in same sc, sc in next sc, *dc in rem lp of next dc in row before last, fpdc around post of next dc in row before last, tr in rem lp of next st in 3rd row below, fpdc around post of next dc in row before last, dc in rem lp of next dc in row before last, sk 5 sc on last row directly behind last 5 sts worked**, sc in each of next 5 sc, rep from * across to last 2 sc, ending last rep at **, sc in each of last 2 sc, turn.

Rows 5 & 6: Rep rows 2 and 3.

Row 7: With C, rep row 4.

Rows 8 & 9: Rep rows 2 and 3.

Row 10: With A, rep row 4.

Row 11: Ch 3, dc in each st across, turn.

Row 12: Ch 1, sc in each dc across, turn.

Row 13: Ch 1, sc in each of first 9 sc, [**sc dec** (see Stitch Guide) in each of next 2 sc, sc in each of next 8 sc] across, turn. (54 sts)

Rows 14–16: Ch 1, sc in each st across, turn.

Row 17: Ch 1, sc in each of first 7 sc, sc dec in next 2 sc, [sc in each of next 7 sc, sc dec in next 2 sc] across, turn. (48 sts)

Rows 18 & 19: Rep row 14. At end of row 19, fasten off. Turn.

Row 20: With size H hook, join B with sl st in first sc, ch 1, sc in same sc, sc in each rem sc across, turn.

Rows 21 & 22: Rep row 14.

Row 23: Ch 1, sc dec in first 2 sc, [sc dec in next 2 sc] across, turn. (24 sts)

Row 24: Rep row 14.

Row 25: Ch 1, sc in each of first 2 sc, sc dec in next 2 sc, [sc in each of next 2 sc, sc dec in next 2 sc] across.

Leaving long length for finishing, fasten off. (18 sts)

Loop Fringe
With size I hook, RS facing, join C with sl st in first st of last row, [ch 12, sl st in next st] across. Fasten off.

Finishing
With tapestry needle, using colors to match sections worked, sew ends of rows tog. With length left for finishing on last row, weave length through sts of last row, pull tightly to gather.

Edging
With RS facing, using size I hook, join A with sl st in first rem lp of foundation ch at base of row 1 of Hat; working in rem lps around, ch 1, [sl st in next st, ch 1] around, join with sl st in beg sl st. Fasten off.

CHILD'S HAT & SCARF FINISHED SIZES
Scarf: 4½ inches wide x 52 inches long not including fringe
Hat: Fits head 19½ inches in diameter

MATERIALS

❑ Medium (worsted) weight yarn (4 oz/200 yds/100g per skein):
  2 skeins lime green (A)
  1 skein each orange (B) and aqua (C)
❑ Size H/8/5mm crochet hook or size needed to obtain gauge
❑ Tapestry needle

GAUGE

13 sc = 4 inches

INSTRUCTIONS

SCARF

First Half

Row 1: With A, ch 16, sc in 2nd ch from hook, sc in each rem ch across, turn. *(15 sc)*

Row 2: Ch 3 *(counts as first dc throughout)*, dc in each sc across, turn.

Row 3: Ch 1, sc in each dc across, turn.

Row 4: Ch 3, dc in each of next 6 sc, dc in front lp only of next sc, dc in each of last 7 sc, turn

Row 5: Ch 1, sc in each of first 5 dc, sc in back lp only of next dc, sc in each of next 3 dc, sc in back lp only of next dc, sc in each of last 5 dc, do not turn. Fasten off.

Row 6 (RS): Join B with a sl st in first sc, ch 1, sc in same sc, sc in each of next 4 sc, dc in rem lp of next dc in row before last, fpdc around post of next dc in row before last, tr in rem lp of next st in 3rd row below, fpdc around post of next dc in row before last, dc in rem lp of next dc in row before last, sk 5 sc on last row directly behind last 5 sts worked, sc in each of last 5 sc, turn.

Row 7: Ch 3, dc in each of next 6 sts, dc in front lp only of next st, dc in each of last 7 sts, turn.

Row 8: Rep row 5.

Rows 9 & 10: With C, rep rows 6 and 7.

Row 11: Rep row 5.

Row 12: With A, rep row 6.

Rows 13–58: Rep rows 2–12 consecutively, ending with a row 3. At end of row 3, do not fasten off. Turn.

Row 59: Ch 3, dc in each dc across, turn.

Row 60: Ch 1, sc in each dc across. Fasten off.

2nd Half

Rows 1–60: Rep rows 1–60 of First Half. At end of row 60, fasten off, leaving length for finishing.

With tapestry needle and length left for finishing, sew last rows of First and 2nd Halves tog through back lps.

Fringe

For each fringe, cut 1 16-inch length strand of each color. Holding all strands tog, fold in half. Insert hook in end st on short edge of either Half, draw folded end through to form lp. Draw loose ends through lp. Pull to tighten. Holding both strands of each color together, braid ends to measure about 1½ inches. Tie knot at end of braid. Rep in every other st across end of Scarf. Trim ends evenly. Rep on rem short edge of Scarf.

HAT

Row 1: With A, ch 60, sc in 2nd ch from hook, sc in each rem ch across, turn. *(59 sc)*

Row 2: Ch 3 *(counts as first dc throughout)*, dc in each of next 3 sc, dc in front lp only of next sc, [dc in each of next 9 sc, dc in front lp only of next sc] across to last 4 sc, dc in each of last 4 sc, turn.

Row 3: Ch 1, sc in each of first 2 dc, sc in back lp only of next dc, sc in each of next 3 dc, sc in back lp only of next dc, [sc in each of next 5 dc, sc in back lp only of next dc, sc in each of next 3 dc, sc in back lp only of next dc] across to last 2 dc, sc in each of last 2 dc. Do not turn. Fasten off.

Row 4 (RS): Join B with sl st in first sc, ch 1, sc in same sc, sc in next sc, *dc in rem lp of next dc in row before last, fpdc around post of next dc in row before last, tr in rem lp of next st in 3rd row below, fpdc around post of next dc in row before last, dc in rem lp of next dc in row before last, sk 5 sc on last row directly behind last 5 sts worked**, sc in each of next 5 sc, rep from * across to last 2 sc, ending last rep at **, sc in each of last 2 sc, turn.

Rows 5 & 6: Rep rows 2 and 3.

Row 7: With C, rep row 4.

Rows 8 & 9: Rep rows 2 and 3.

Row 10: With A, rep row 4.

Row 11: Ch 3, dc in each st across, turn.

Row 12: Ch 3, sc in each dc across, turn.

Row 13: Ch 1, sc in each of first 9 sc, [sc dec in each of next 2 sc, sc in each of next 8 sc] across, turn. *(54 sts)*

Rows 14–16: Ch 1, sc in each st across, turn.

Row 17: Ch 1, sc in each of first 7 sc, sc dec in next 2 sc, [sc in each of next 7 sc, sc dec in next 2 sc] across, turn. *(48 sts)*

Rows 18 & 19: Rep row 14. At end of row 19, fasten off. Turn.

Row 20: Join B with sl st in first sc, ch 1, sc in same sc, sc in each rem sc across, turn.

Rows 21 & 22: Rep row 14.

Row 23: Ch 1, sc dec in first 2 sc, [sc dec in next 2 sc] across, turn. *(24 sts)*

Row 24: Rep row 14.

Row 25: Rep row 23. Leaving long length for finishing, fasten off. *(18 sts)*

Fringe

Rep instructions for Scarf Fringe in each st across last row of Hat.

Finishing

With tapestry needle, using colors to match sections worked, sew ends of rows tog. With length left for finishing on last row, weave length through sts of last row, pull tightly to gather.

Edging

With RS facing, join A with sl st in first rem lp of foundation ch at base of row 1 of Hat; working in rem lps around, ch 1, [sl st in next st, ch 1] around, join with sl st in beg sl st. Fasten off. ❑❑

Convertible Mittens

Design by Kathleen Stuart

SKILL LEVEL

EASY

FINISHED SIZES

Child's palm width: 2½ inches
Adult's palm width: 3 inches
Instructions are given for child's size; changes for adult's size are in [ ]. When only 1 number is given it applies to both sizes.

MATERIALS

- ❑ Medium (worsted) weight yarn:
  3 [5] oz/150 [250] yds/85 [142] g
- ❑ Size G/6/4mm crochet hook or size needed to obtain gauge
- ❑ Yarn needle
- ❑ Safety pins or other small markers

GAUGE

5 sc = 1 inch

INSTRUCTIONS

MITTEN
Make 2.

Right Palm

Rnd 1: Ch 30 [36], join with sl st to form ring, ch 3 *(counts as first dc throughout),* dc in each rem ch around, join with sl st in 3rd ch of beg ch-3. *(30 [36] dc)*

Rnds 2–5 [2–8]: Ch 2 *(counts as first bpdc),* **fpdc** *(see Stitch Guide)* around post of each of next 2 sts, [**bpdc** *(see Stitch Guide)* around post of next st, fpdc around post of each of next 2 sts] around, join with sl st in 2nd ch of beg ch-2.

Note: *Do not join rem rnds unless otherwise stated. Mark first st of each rnd with safety pin or other small marker.*

Rnd 6 [9]: Ch 1, sc in same st as joining, sc in each of next 3 [4] sts, 2 sc in next st, [sc in each of next 4 (5) sts, 2 sc in next st] around. *(36 [42] sc)*

Rnd 7–13 [10–19]: [Sc in **front lp** *(see Stitch Guide)* only of next st, sc in **back lp** *(see Stitch Guide)* only of next st] around.

Rnd 14 [20]: Ch 6, sk next 10 sc for thumb opening, [sc in front lp only of next sc, sc in back lp only of next sc] around.

Rnd 15 [21]: Sc in each of next 6 chs, [sc in front lp only of next sc, sc in back lp only of next sc] around. *(32 [38] sc)*

Rnd(s) 16 [22 & 23]: Rep rnd(s) 7 [13 and 14].

Rnd 17 [24]: Working in back lps only, sc in each sc around, marking rem lp of next-to-last sc on rnd 16 [23].

Rnds 18 & 19 [25–27]: Rep rnds 7 and 8 [13–15]. Do not fasten off at end of rnd 19 [27].

Right Convertible Glove
First finger

Rnd 1: Sc in each of next 4 [5] sc of rnd 19 [27] *(mark st on rnd 19 [27] into which last sc was made)*, ch 3, sk next 24 [29] sc, sc in each of last 4 sc. *(8 [9] sc, 3 chs)*

Rnd 2: Sc in each sc and ch around. *(11 [12] sc)*

Rnds 3–4 [3–6]: Sc in each sc around. At end of rnd 4 [6], join with sl st in beg sc. Fasten off.

2nd finger

Rnd 1: Join yarn with sl st in marked sc on rnd 19 [27], sc in each of next 4 [5] unworked sc *(mark st on rnd 19 [27] into which last sc was made)*, ch 3, sc in each of last 4 [5] unworked sc of rnd 19 [27], sc in rem lp of each of next 3 chs of ch-3 of previous finger. *(11 [13] sc, 3 chs)*

Rnd 2: Rep rnd 2 of previous finger. *(14 [16] sc)*

Rnd 3–4 [3–6]: Rep rnds 3–4 [3–6] of First Finger.

3rd finger

Rnds 1–4 [1–6]: Rep rnds 1–4 [1–6] of 2nd Finger.

4th finger

Rnd 1: Join yarn with sl st in marked sc on rnd 19 [27], sc in each of next 8 [9] unworked sc, sc in rem lp of each of next 3 chs of ch-3 of previous finger. *(11 [12] sc)*

Rnds 2–3 [2–5]: Sc in each sc around. At end of rnd 3 [5], fasten off.

Right Thumb

Rnd 1: Join yarn with sl st in first sk sc of rnd 13 [19], ch 1, sc in same sc, sc in each of next 9 sc, sc in each rem lp of ch-6. *(16 sc)*

Child's Size Only

Rnd 2: Sc in each sc around.

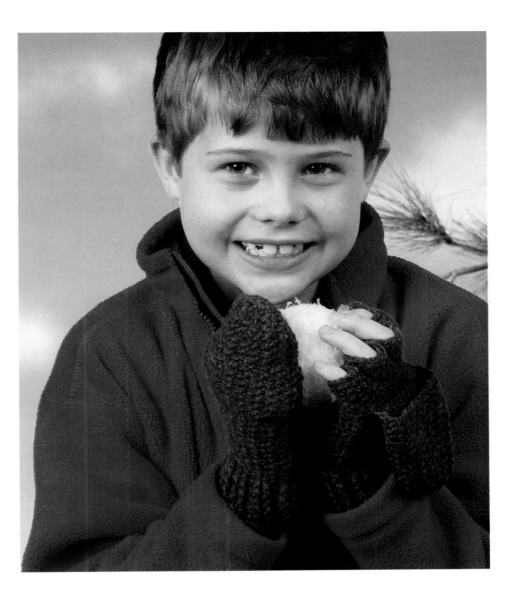

Rnd 3: [Sc in each of next 6 sc, **sc dec** *(see Stitch Guide)* in next 2 sc] twice. *(14 sts)*

Rnds 4–10: Sc in each st around.

Rnd 11: [Sc dec in next 2 sc] around, join with sl st in beg sc dec. Leaving short length for finishing, fasten off. With yarn needle, weave length left for finishing through sts of last rnd, pull to close opening. Fasten off.

Adult's Size Only

Rnds 2–13: Sc in each sc around.

Rnd 14: [Sc in each of next 2 sts, sc dec in next 2 sts] around. *(12 sts)*

Rnd 15: [Sc in next st, sc dec in next 2 sts] around, join with sl st in beg sc. Leaving short length for finishing, fasten off. With yarn needle, weave length for finishing through sts of last rnd, pull to close opening. Fasten off.

Right Mitten Top

Rnd 1: Join yarn with sl st in marked rem lp of rnd 16 [23], ch 19 [23], sk next 18 [22] rem lps, sc in each of next 13 [15] rem lps, sc in each of next 19 [23] chs. *(32 [38] sc)*

Rnds 2–11 [2–17]: [Sc in front lp only of next sc, sc in back lp only of next sc] around.

Adult's Size Only

Rnd 18: Continuing in established pattern of alternate front and back lps, sc in next sc, [sc in each of next 4 sc, sc dec in next 2 sc] around, ending with sc in last sc. *(32 sts)*

All Sizes

Rnd 12 [19]: Continuing in established pattern of alternate front and back lps, sc in next st, [sc in each of next 3 sts, sc dec in next 2 sts] around,

ending with sc in last st. *(26 sts)*

Rnd 13 [20]: Continuing in established pattern of alternate front and back lps, sc in next st, [sc in each of next 2 sts, sc dec in next 2 sts] around, ending with sc in last st. *(20 sts)*

Rnd 14 [21]: Continuing in established pattern of alternate front and back lps, sc in next st, [sc in next st, sc dec in next 2 sts] around, ending with sc in last st. Leaving short length for finishing, fasten off. *(14 sts)*

With yarn needle, weave length for finishing through sts of last rnd, pull to close opening. Fasten off.

Left Palm
Rnds 1–16 [1–23]: Rep rnds 1–19 [1–27] of Right Palm.

Rnd 17 [24]: Working in back lps only, sc in each sc around, marking rem lp of 19th [23rd] sc on rnd 16 [23].

Rnds 18–19 [25–27]: Rep rnds 18–19 [25–27] of Right Palm.

Left Convertible Glove
First Finger
Rnd 1: Sc in each of next 8 [9] sc of rnd 19 [27] (mark st on rnd 19 [27] into which last sc was made), ch 3. (8 [9] sc, 3 chs)

Rnd 2: Sc in each of next 8 [9] sc, sc in each of next 3 chs. *(11 [12] sc)*

Rnds 3–4 [6]: Rep rnds 3–4 [6] of First Finger for Right Fingerless Glove.

2nd Finger
Rnds 1–4 [6]: Rep rnds 1–4 [6] of 2nd Finger for Right Fingerless Glove.

3rd Finger
Rnds 1–4 [6]: Rep rnds 1–4 [6] of 3rd Finger for Right Fingerless Glove.

4th Finger
Rnds 1–3 [1–5]: Rep rnds 1–3 [1–5] of 4th Finger for Right Fingerless Glove.

Left Thumb
Rnds 1–11 [1–15]: Rep rnds 1–11 [1–15] of Right Thumb for Right Fingerless Glove.

Left Mitten Top
Rnds 1–21: Rep rnds 1–21 of Right Mitten Top. ❑❑

Fantastic for Fall Shawl & Cloche

Designs by Katherine Eng courtesy of Lion Brand Yarn

SKILL LEVEL

INTERMEDIATE

FINISHED SIZES
Shawl: 16 x 70 inches not including fringe
Cloche: One size fits most adults

MATERIALS
❑ Lion Brand Homespun bulky (chunky) weight yarn (6 oz/185 yds/170g per skein): 3 skeins #307 antique (MC) and 1 skein #345 Corinthian (CC)
❑ Size H/8/5mm crochet hook or size needed to obtain gauge
❑ Tapestry needle

GAUGE
6 sc, 3 ch-2 sps, 3 ch-3 sps worked in pattern = 4½ inches; 9 rows sc = 4 inches

INSTRUCTIONS
SHAWL
First Half
Note: *When joining new color or fastening off, leave 7-inch lengths to be worked into Fringe.*

Row 1 (RS): With MC, ch 186, (sc, ch 2, sc) in 2nd ch from hook, [ch 3, sk 3 chs, (sc, ch 2, sc) in next ch] across, turn. *(47 ch-2 sps, 46 ch-3 sps)*

Row 2: Ch 1, (sc, ch 2, sc) in first ch-2 sp, [ch 3, (sc, ch 2, sc) in next ch-2 sp] across, turn. Fasten off.

Row 3: Join CC with sl st in first ch-2 sp, ch 1, (sc, ch 2, sc) in same sp, [ch 3, (sc, ch 2, sc) in next ch-2 sp] across, turn. Fasten off.

Row 4: With MC, rep row 3. Do not fasten off. Turn.

Rows 5–7: Rep row 4. At end of row 7, fasten off. Turn.

Rows 8–18: Rep rows 3–17 consecutively, ending with a row 3.

2nd Half
Row 1: With RS facing, join MC with sl st in first rem lp of foundation ch at base of row 1 of First Half, ch 1, (sc, ch 2, sc) in same st; working in rem lps across, [ch 3, sk 3 chs, (sc, ch 2, sc) in next ch] across, turn.

Rows 2–18: Rep rows 2–18 of First Half.

Fringe
For each Fringe, cut strand of yarn 14

inches long. Fold strand in half, insert hook in end of row, draw fold end through to form lp, draw loose ends and 7-inch length left for finishing through lp, pull to tighten. Trim ends evenly.

Matching color to row being worked, work Fringe in end of each row across both short ends of Shawl.

CLOCHE
Rnd 1 (RS): With CC, ch 4, join with sl st to form ring, ch 1, (sc, ch 2, sc) 8 times in ring, join with sl st in beg sc. *(8 ch-2 sps)*

Rnd 2: (Sl st, ch 1, sc, ch 2, sc) in first sp, (sc, ch 2, sc) in each rem sp around, join with sl st in beg sc.

Rnd 3: (Sl st, ch 1, sc, ch 2, sc) in first sp, ch 1, [(sc, ch 2, sc) in next sp, ch 1] around, join with sl st in beg sc. *(8 ch-2 sps, 8 ch-1 sps)*

Rnd 4: (Sl st, ch 1, sc, ch 2, sc) in first sp, (sc, ch 3, sc) in next sp, [(sc, ch 2, sc) in next sp, (sc, ch 3, sc) in next sp] around, join with sl st in beg sc. *(8 ch-2 sps, 8 ch-3 sps)*

Rnds 5 & 6: Rep rnds 2 and 3. *(32 ch sps at end of rnd 6)*

Rnds 8–10: (Sl st, ch 1, sc, ch 2, sc) in first sp, ch 2, sk next sp, [(sc, ch 2, sc) in next sp, ch 2, sk next sp] around, join with sl st in beg sc.

Rnds 11 & 12: (Sl st, ch 1, sc, ch 2, sc) in first sp, ch 3, sk next sp, [(sc, ch 2, sc) in next sp, ch 3, sk next sp] around, join with sl st in beg sc. At end of rnd 12, fasten off.

Rnd 13: With RS facing, join MC with sl st in first sp, ch 1, (sc, ch 2, sc) in same sp, ch 3, sk next sp, [(sc, ch 2, sc) in next sp, ch 3, sk next sp] around, join with sl st in beg sc.

Rnds 14 & 15: Rep rnds 11 and 12.

Rnd 16: With RS facing, join CC with sl st in first sp, ch 1, (sc, ch 2, sc) in same sp, ch 2, sk next sp, [(sc, ch 2, sc) in next sp, ch 2, sk next sp] around, join with sl st in beg sc.

Rnd 17: Rep rnd 8. Fasten off. ❑❑

Soft, snuggly afghans are always appreciated for their decorative appeal and functional versatility. They warm the body and beautify the home, and touch the hearts of all who receive them—whatever the occasion, whatever the reason.

Aspen Twist Afghan

Design by Glenda Winkleman

SKILL LEVEL

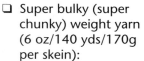

BEGINNER

FINISHED SIZE

45 inches x 64 inches

MATERIALS

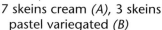

SUPER BULKY

- Super bulky (super chunky) weight yarn (6 oz/140 yds/170g per skein):
  7 skeins cream *(A)*, 3 skeins pastel variegated *(B)*
- Size M/13/9mm crochet hook or size needed to obtain gauge

GAUGE

4 sc = 2 inches; 4 sc rows = 2 inches

SPECIAL STITCH

Picot: Ch 3, sl st in top of last dc made.

INSTRUCTIONS

AFGHAN

Row 1(RS): With A, ch 130, sc in 2nd ch from hook, sc in each rem ch across, turn. *(129 sc)*

Row 2: Ch 1, sc in first sc, [ch 1, sk next sc, sc in next sc] across, turn. *(65 sc, 64 ch-1 sps)*

Row 3: Ch 1, sc in first sc, [ch 1, sc in next sc] across, turn.

Row 4: Ch 1, sc in each sc and each ch-1 sp across, turn. *(129 sc)*

Rows 5–94: Rep rows 2–4. At end of row 94, fasten off.

Woven Strip

Make 16.

With B, leaving a 6-inch length for finishing, ch 195, leave 6-inch length for finishing, fasten off.

Each Strip is woven through ch-1 sps of rows 2 and 3 of every other rep across. With RS facing, beg in first ch-1 sp of row 2, bring Strip up through first sp of row 2 and down through next ch-1 sp of row 3, [bring Strip up through next sp of row 2 and down through next sp of row 3] across. Secure beg and end of Strip with lengths left for finishing.

Beg in row 8, rep instructions for first Strip with next Strip, weaving through ch-1 sps of rows 8 and 9. Continue across in every other rep of rows 2 and 3.

Border

With RS facing, join B with a sl st in first st at right-hand corner of last row, ch 3 *(counts as first dc)*; working across last row, dc in next st, **picot** *(see Special Stitch)*, *[dc in each of next 2 sts, picot] across to last st, (2 dc, picot) in last st, dc over end st of each of next 2 rows, picot, dc over end st of next row, sk next row, dc over end st of next row, picot] across to last row, (2 dc, picot) over end st of last row, rep from * around, join with sl st in 3rd ch of beg ch-3. Fasten off. ❑❑

Compassion is a network of invisible threads that weave a blanket of love around many lives.

—Unknown

Fallen Petals

Design by Lisa Thomm

SKILL LEVEL

EASY

FINISHED SIZE
48 x 66 inches

MATERIALS

❑ TLC Essentials medium (worsted) weight yarn (6 oz/326 yds/170g per skein):
   8 skeins #2531 light plum
❑ Size L/11/8mm crochet hook or size needed to obtain gauge
❑ Yarn needle

GAUGE
With 2 strands held tog: (shell, sc, 2 ch-2 sps) in pattern = 3½ inches

SPECIAL STITCH
Shell: 4 tr in indicated st.

INSTRUCTIONS

AFGHAN
Row 1(RS): With 2 strands held tog, ch 98, sc in 2nd ch from hook, [ch 2, sk 3 chs, **shell** (see Special Stitch) in next ch, ch 2, sk 3 chs, sc in next ch] across, turn. (12 shells, 13 sc, 24 ch-2 sps)

Row 2: Ch 1, sc in first sc, [ch 3, sk next tr, sc in next tr, ch 3, sk 2 tr, sc in next sc] across, turn. (25 sc, 24 ch-3 sps)

Row 3: Ch 4 (counts as first tr throughout), tr in first sc, ch 2, sc in next sc, ch 2, [shell in next sc, ch 2, sc in next sc, ch 2] across to last sc, 2 tr in last sc, turn. (11 shells)

Row 4: Ch 1, sc in first tr, ch 3, sk next tr, sc in next sc, ch 3, sk next tr, [sc in next tr, ch 3, sk next 2 tr, sc in next sc, ch 3, sk next tr] across to beg ch-4, sc in 4th ch of beg ch-4, turn.

Row 5: Ch 1, sc in first sc, [ch 2, shell in next sc, ch 2, sc in next sc] across, turn. (12 shells)

Rows 6–74: Rep rows 2–5 consecutively, ending with a row 2. At end of row 74, do not fasten off. Turn.

Border
Rnd 1 (RS): Ch 1, 3 sc in first sc, *[4 sc in next ch-3 sp, 3 sc in next ch-3 sp]* across to last sc of row 74, 3 sc in last sc; **working over end sts of rows, sc over each ending sc, 3 sc over each ending tr across to next corner**, 3 sc in corner; working in rem lps across foundation ch, rep bet * across to next corner, 3 sc in corner st, rep bet **, join with sl st in beg sc. (398 sc)

Rnd 2: Ch 1, sc in first sc, *[ch 5, sc in next sc] twice, ch 5 sk next 4 sc, [sc in next sc, ch 5, sk next 4 sc] across to next 3-sc corner group, sc in next sc, [ch 5, sc in next sc] twice, ch 4, sk next sc, [sc in next sc, ch 5, sk next 4 sc] across to next 3-sc corner group, rep from * around, join with sl st in beg sc. (2 ch-5 sps at each corner, 17 ch-5 lps at top and bottom, 22 ch-5 lps across each side)

Rnd 3: Sl st in each of first 2 chs, (sl st, ch 1, sc, ch 3, sc) in next ch, ch 5, [(sc, ch 3, sc) in 3rd ch of next ch-5, ch 5] around, join with sl st in beg sc.

Rnds 4–6: Sl st in each of next 3 chs, in next sc and in each of first 2 chs of next ch-5, (sl st, ch 1, sc, ch 3, sc) in next ch of same ch-5, ch 5, [(sc, ch 3, sc) in 3rd ch of next ch-5, ch 5] around, join with sl st in beg sc.

Rnd 7: (Sl st, ch 1, sc, {ch 3, sc} twice) in next ch-3 sp, ch 2, sc in 3rd ch of next ch-5, ch 2, *(sc, {ch 3, sc} twice) in next ch-3 sp, ch 2, sc in 3rd ch of next ch-5, ch 2, rep from * around, join with sl st in beg sc. Fasten off. ❑❑

Summer Skies Afghan

Design by Carol Alexander

SKILL LEVEL

EASY

FINISHED SIZE
48 x 65 inches

MATERIALS

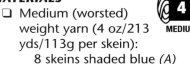

- ❑ Medium (worsted) weight yarn (4 oz/213 yds/113g per skein): 8 skeins shaded blue *(A)*
- ❑ Medium (worsted) weight yarn (3½ oz/190 yds/99g per skein): 10 skeins medium blue *(B)*
- ❑ Size N/15/10mm crochet hook or size needed to obtain gauge
- ❑ Yarn needle

GAUGE
On row 1, with 1 strand each A and B held together: (shell, V-st) in pattern = 3½ inches

SPECIAL STITCHES
Shell: 7 dc in indicated st.
V-stitch (V-st): (Dc, ch 2, dc) in indicated st or sp.
Picot: Ch 3, sc around **post** *(see Stitch Guide)* of last dc made.
Picot shell: (Dc, picot, {2 dc, picot} twice) in indicated st or sp.
Beginning picot shell (beg picot shell): (Ch 6, sl st in 3rd ch from hook, {2 dc, **picot** *(see Special Stitches)*} twice) in indicated st or sp.

INSTRUCTIONS

AFGHAN
Row 1: With 1 strand each A and B held tog, ch 125, dc in 5th ch from hook, *sk 4 chs, **shell** *(see Special Stitches)* in next ch, sk 4 chs**, **V-st** *(see Special Stitches)* in next ch, rep from * across, ending last rep at **, (dc, ch 1, dc) in last ch, turn. *(12 shells)*

Row 2: Ch 4 *(counts as first dc, ch-1 throughout)*, dc in first dc, *sk first dc of next shell, dc in each of next 5 dc**, V-st in next V-st sp, rep from * across, ending last rep at **, (dc, ch 1, dc) in 3rd ch of beg ch-4, turn.

Row 3: Ch 3 *(counts as first dc throughout)*, 3 dc in ch-1 sp, *V-st in 3rd dc of next 5-dc group**, shell in next V-st sp, rep from * across, ending last rep at **, 3 dc in turning ch-4 sp, dc in 3rd ch of same beg ch-4, turn. *(11 shells)*

Row 4: Ch 3, dc in each of next 2 dc, *V-st in next V-st sp**, sk first dc of next shell, dc in each of next 5 dc, rep from * across, ending last rep at **, sk next dc, dc in each of next 2 dc, dc in 3rd ch of beg ch-3, turn.

Row 5: Ch 4, dc in first dc, *shell in next V-st sp**, V-st in 3rd dc of next 5-dc group, rep from * across, ending last rep at **, (dc, ch 1, dc) in 3rd ch of beg ch-3, turn. *(12 shells)*

Rows 6–64: Rep rows 2–5 consecutively, ending with a row 4. At end of row 64, do not fasten off. Turn.

Border
Rnd 1 (RS): Ch 1, 3 sc in corner st, sc evenly around afghan, working 3 sc in each corner st and having equal number of sc on opposite sides, join with sl st in beg sc.

Rnd 2: Sl st in next sc, ch 1, 3 sc in same st, sc in each rem sc around, working 3 sc in each corner sc, join with sl st in beg sc.

Rnd 3: (Sl st, **beg picot shell**—*see Special Stitches*) in next sc, *ch 1, sk 2 sc, sc in next sc, [ch 1, sk 3 sc, **picot shell** *(see Special Stitches)* in next sc, ch 1, sk 3 sc, sc in next sc] across to 3rd sc from next corner, adjusting number of sts sk if necessary, ch 1, sk 2 sc**, picot shell in corner sc, rep from * around, ending last rep at **, join in 3rd ch of beg ch-3. Fasten off.

Tassel
Make 1 for each picot shell across each short end of afghan including corner picot shells.

Cut 12, 12-inch lengths each of A and B for each Tassel. Holding all strands tog, tie tightly together in center using a separate length of yarn. Leave ends of separate length at top of Tassel uncut for finishing. Fold lengths in half at tied section. Tie another 12-inch length of yarn around Tassel 1¼ inches from folded top. Trim ends evenly. Using ends left for finishing at top of Tassel, tie 1 Tassel to center picot of each picot shell across each short end of Afghan. ❑❑

Every newborn is a heavenly gift of humanity at its best. Celebrating the arrival of a new baby is one of life's happiest occasions and this enchanting collection of projects for babies from preemies to 12 months is sure to delight the tiny treasures in your life.

Ombré Waves Sweater

Design by Lori Zeller

SKILL LEVEL

INTERMEDIATE

FINISHED SIZES

Infants 3–6 mos (small) and 9–12 mos (large)
Instructions are given for size small; changes for large are in [ ]. When only one number is given it applies to both sizes.

MATERIALS

- ❏ Fine (sport) weight yarn (2½ oz/240 yds/70g per skein):
  2 skeins baby pastel ombré (MC)
  1 skein white (CC)
- ❏ Sizes E/4/3.5mm and G/6/4mm crochet hooks or size needed to obtain gauge
- ❏ Tapestry needle
- ❏ Sewing needle and white sewing thread
- ❏ 3 size 1/0 snaps
- ❏ 3 gold 10 x 15mm shank buttons
- ❏ Safety pins or other small markers

GAUGE

Size G hook: 4 sc = 1 inch; 4 pattern rows = 1 inch

INSTRUCTIONS

SWEATER BODY

First Half

Row 1 (RS): With size G hook and MC, beg at center back, ch 33 [45], sc in 2nd ch from hook, sc in next ch, dc in each of next 2 chs, [sc in each of next 2 chs, dc in each of next 2 chs] across, turn. *(32 [44] sts)*

Rows 2–17 [2–19]: Ch 1, [sc in each of next 2 dc, dc in each of next 2 sc] across, turn.

Divide for Back and First Front

Row 18 [20]: Ch 1, [sc in each of next 2 dc, dc in each of next 2 sc] across first 16 [24] sts, place marker in last st made, leave rem 16 [20] sts unworked, turn.

Row 19 [21]: Beg at shoulder edge, ch 17 [21], sc in 2nd ch from hook, sc in next ch, dc in each of next 2 chs, [sc in each of next 2 chs, dc in each of next 2 chs] across to next dc, [sc in each of next 2 dc, dc in each of next 2 sc] across, turn. *(32 [44] sts)*

Rows 20–26 [22–30]: Rep row 2.

Neck Shaping

Row 27 [31]: Ch 1, **sc dec** *(see Stitch Guide)* in first 2 sts, dc in each of next 2 sc, [sc in each of next 2 dc, dc in each of next 2 sc] across, turn. *(31 [43] sts)*

Row 28 [32]: Ch 1, [sc in each of next 2 dc, dc in each of next 2 sc] across to last 3 sts, sc dec in next 2 sts, dc in last st, turn. *(30 [42] sts)*

Row 29 [33]: Ch 1, sc dec in first 2 sts, sc dec in next 2 sts, dc in each of next 2 sc, [sc in each of next 2 dc, dc in each of next 2 sc] across, turn. *(28 [40] sts)*

Row 30 [34]: Ch 1, [sc in each of next 2 dc, dc in each of next 2 sc] across to last 4 sts, sc dec in next 2 sts, dc each of next 2 sts, turn. *(27 [39] sts)*

Row 31 [35]: Ch 1, sc dec in first 2 sts, dc in next st, [sc in each of next 2 dc, dc in each of next 2 sc] across, turn. *(26 [38] sts)*

Row 32 [36]: Ch 1, [sc in each of next 2 dc, dc in each of next 2 sc] across to last 2 sts, sc dec in last 2 sts, turn. *(25 [37] sts)*

Row 33 [37]: Ch 1, sc dec in first 2 sts, sc in next dc, dc in each of next 2 sc, [sc in each of next 2 dc, dc in each of next 2 sc] across, turn. *(24 [36] sts)*

Row 34 [38]: Ch 1, [sc in each of next 2 sts, dc in each of next 2 sts] across. Fasten off.

2nd Half

Row 1: Beg at waist edge, working in rem lps across opposite side of foundation ch at base of row 1 on First Half, join MC with a sl st in first st, ch 1, sc in same st, sc in next st, dc in each of next 2 sts, [sc in each of next 2 sts, dc in each of next 2 sts] across, turn. *(32 [44] sts)*

Rows 2–17 [2–19]: Rep rows 2-17 [19] of First Half. At end of row 17 [19], fasten off. Turn.

Divide for Back & 2nd Front

Row 18 [20]: With MC ch 16 [20], sk last 16 [20] sts of last row, sc in next dc, place marker in this sc, sc in next dc, dc in each of next 2 sc, [sc in each of next 2 dc, dc in each of next 2 sc] across, turn.

Row 19 [21]: Ch 1, [sc in each of next 2 dc, dc in each of next 2 sc] across to first ch, [sc in each of next 2 chs, dc in each of next 2 chs] across, turn. *(32 [44] sts)*

Rows 20–26 [22–30]: Rep rows 20 [22]–26 [30] of First Half.

Neck Shaping

Row 27 [31]: Ch 1, [sc in each of next 2 dc, dc in each of next 2 sc] across to last 4 sts, sc dec in each of next 2 sts, dc in each of last 2 sts, turn. *(31 [43] sts)*

Row 28 [32]: Ch 1, sc dec in first 2 sts, sk next st, [sc in each of next 2 dc, dc in each of next 2 sc] across, turn. *(29 [41] sts)*

Row 29 [33]: Ch 1, [sc in each of next 2 dc, dc in each of next 2 sc] across to last 5 sts, sc in next st, sc

dec in next 2 sts, dc in each of last 2 sts, turn. *(28 [40] sts)*

Row 30 [34]: Ch 1, sc dec in first 2 sts, dc in each of next 2 sts, [sc in each of next 2 dc, dc in each of next 2 sc] across, turn. *(27 [39] sts)*

Row 31 [35]: Ch 1, [sc in each of next 2 dc, dc in each of next 2 sc] across to last 3 sts, sk next st, **dc dec** *(see Stitch Guide)* in last 2 sts, turn. *(25 [37] sts)*

Row 32 [36]: Ch 1, sc dec in first 2 sts, sc in next st, dc in each of next 2 sc, [sc in each of next 2 dc, dc in each of next 2 sc] across, turn. *(24 [36] sts)*

Rows 33 & 34 [37 & 38]: Ch 1, [sc in each of next 2 sts, dc in each of next 2 sts] across, turn. At end of row 34 [38], fasten off.

With tapestry needle and MC, sew shoulder seams.

Edging

With size G hook, join MC with sl st over end st of row at center back neck, ch 1; beg in same st, sc evenly sp across neck, down First Front, across bottom, up 2nd Front and across rem half of neck, working 3 sc in each corner; join with sl st in beg sc. Fasten off.

Ribbing

Row 1: With size E hook, join CC with sl st in first sc of Edging, ch 5, sc in 2nd ch from hook, sc in each of next 3 chs, sl st in each of next 2 sc on Edging, turn. *(4 sc)*

Row 2: Ch 1; working in **back lps** *(see Stitch Guide)* only, sk sl sts, sc in each of next 4 sc, turn.

Row 3: Ch 1; working in back lps only, sc in each of next 4 sc, sl st in each of next 2 sc on Edging, turn.

Rep rows 2 and 3 around entire sweater, working row 3 with sl st in only 1 st on Edging and in each 3 corner sts of each corner, ending with a row 2. Fasten off, leaving short length for finishing.

With tapestry needle and length left for finishing, sew first and last rows of Ribbing tog.

First Sleeve

Row 1: With size G hook and WS facing, join MC with sl st around

post of marked st on row 18 [20] of First Half of body, ch 3 *(counts as first dc throughout)*, dc in same st; beg with sc and working in established pattern of [2 sc, 2 dc], work 36 [44] more sts evenly sp around, turn. *(38 [46] sts)*

Row 2: Ch 1, sc in each of first 2 sts, [dc in each of next 2 sc, sc in each of next 2 dc] across, turn.

Row 3: Ch 3, dc in next sc, [sc in each of next 2 dc, dc in each of next 2 sc] across, turn.

Rows 4–7 [4–9]: Rep rows 2 and 3 alternately.

Row 8 [10]: Ch 1, sc dec in first 2 dc, dc in each of next 2 sc, [sc in each of next 2 dc, dc in each of next 2 sc] across to last 2 dc, sc dec in last 2 dc, turn. *(36 [44] sts)*

Row 9 [11]: Ch 1, sc dec in first 2 sts, sc in next st, [dc in each of next 2 sc, sc in each of next 2 dc] across to last 3 sts, sc in next st, sc dec in last 2 sts, turn. *(34 [42] sts)*

Row 10 [12]: Ch 3, dc in next sc, sc in each of next 2 dc, [dc in each of next 2 sc, sc in each of next 2 dc] across to last 2 sts, dc in each of last 2 sts, turn.

Rows 11–13 [13–19]: Rep rows 2 and 3 alternately, ending with a row 2.

Rows 14 & 15 [20 & 21]: Ch 1, sc dec in first 2 sts, sc dec in next 2 sts, dc in each of next 2 sts, [sc in each of next 2 sts, dc in each of next 2 sts] across to last 4 sts, [sc dec in next 2 sts] twice, turn. *(26 [34] sts at end of row 15 [21])*

Row 16 [22]: Ch 3, dc in next st, sc in each of next 2 dc, [dc in each of next 2 sc, sc in each of next 2 dc] across to last 2 sts, dc in each of last 2 sts, turn.

Row 17 [23]: Ch 1, sc dec in first 2 dc, dc in each of next 2 sc, [sc in each of next 2 dc, dc in each of next 2 sc] across to last 2 dc, sc dec in last 2 dc, turn. *(24 [32] sts)*

Row 18 [24]: Ch 1, sc dec in first 2 sts, sc in next dc, dc in each of next 2 sc, [sc in each of next 2 dc, dc in each of next 2 sc] across to last 3 sts, sc in next st, sc dec in last 2 sts. Fasten off, leaving length for finishing. *(22 [30] sts)*

With tapestry needle and length left for finishing, sew Sleeve seam.

Ribbing

Row 1: With size E hook, join CC with sl st in any st around wrist opening, ch 5, sc in 2nd ch from hook, sc in each of next 3 chs, sl st in each of next 2 sts on Sleeve, turn. *(4 sc)*

Row 2: Ch 1; working in back lps (see Stitch Guide) only, sk sl sts, sc in each of next 4 sc, turn.

Row 3: Ch 1; working in back lps only, sc in each of next 4 sc, sl st in each of next 2 sts on Sleeve, turn.

Rep rows 2 and 3 around, ending with a row 2. Fasten off, leaving short length for finishing.

With tapestry needle and length left for finishing, sew first and last rows of Ribbing tog.

2nd Sleeve

Row 1: With size G hook and WS facing, join MC with sl st around post of marked st on row 18[20] of First Half of body, ch 1 sc in same st, sc in next st; beg with dc and working in established pattern of [2 dc, 2 sc], work 36 [44] more sts evenly sp around, turn. *(38 [46] sts)*

Row 2: Ch 3, dc in next sc, [sc in each of next 2 dc, dc in each of next 2 sc] across, turn.

Row 3: Ch 1, sc in each of first 2 dc, [dc in each of next 2 sc, sc in each of next 2 dc] across, turn.

Rows 4–7 [9]: Rep rows 2 and 3 alternately.

Row 8 [10]: Ch 3, dc in next dc, sc dec in next 2 dc, dc in each of next 2 sc, [sc in each of next 2 dc, dc in each of next 2 sc] across to last 4 sts, sc dec in next 2 sts, dc in each of last 2 sts, turn. *(36 [44] sts)*

Row 9 [11]: Ch 1, sc dec in first 2 sts, dc in next st, sc in each of next 2 dc, [dc in each of next 2 sc, sc in each of next 2 dc] across to last 3 sts, dc in next st, sc dec in last 2 sts, turn. *(34 [42] sts)*

Row 10 [12]: Ch 1, sc in each of first 2 sts, dc in each of next 2 sc, [sc in each of next 2 dc, dc in each of next 2 sc] across to last 2 sts, sc in each of last 2 sts, turn.

Rows 11–13 [13–19]: Rep rows 2 & 3 alternately, ending with a row 2.

Row 14 & 15 [20 & 21]: Ch 1, sc dec in first 2 sts, sk next st, dc in next st, sc in each of next 2 dc, [dc in each of next 2 sc, sc in each of next 2 dc] across to last 4 sts, sk next st, dc in next st, sc dec in last 2 sts, turn. *(26 [34] sts)*

Row 16 [22]: Ch 1, sc in each of first 2 sts, dc in each of next 2 sc, [sc in each of next 2 dc, dc in each of next 2 sc] across to last 2 sts, sc in each of last 2 sts, turn.

Row 17 [23]: Ch 3, dc in next st, sc dec in next 2 dc, dc in each of next 2 sc, [sc in each of next 2 dc, dc in each of next 2 sc] across to last 4 sts, sc dec in next 2 sts, dc in each of last 2 sts, turn. *(24 [32] sts)*

Row 18 [24]: Ch 1, sc dec in first 2 sts, dc in next st, sc in each of next 2 dc, [dc in each of next 2 sc, sc in each of next 2 dc] across to last 3 sts, dc in next st, sc dec in last 2 sts. Fasten off, leaving length for finishing. *(22 [30] sts)*

With tapestry needle and length left for finishing, sew Sleeve seam.

Ribbing

Rows 1–3: Rep rows 1–3 of Ribbing for First Sleeve.

Finishing

Sew 3 snaps evenly spaced down one Front. Sew buttons over snaps on RS of Ribbing. ❑❑

You come with a birthright, written in love, which promises that no matter where you're at, you are home; that no matter who you're with, you are welcome; that no matter who you are, you are loved.

—Rita Ramsey

Baby Mittens

Design by Shirley Patterson

SKILL LEVEL

□■□□

BEGINNER

FINISHED SIZE

0–3 months

MATERIALS

- ❑ Fingering (super fine) 3-ply yarn (1¾ oz/259 yds/50g per skein): 1 skein white
- ❑ Size E/4/3.5mm crochet hook or size needed to obtain gauge
- ❑ Tapestry needle
- ❑ Sewing needle
- ❑ Sewing thread
- ❑ 28-inch length ⅛-inch-wide blue satin ribbon
- ❑ 2 blue satin ribbon rosebuds

GAUGE

5 hdc = 1 inch

INSTRUCTIONS

Mitten Half

Make 4.

Row 1: Ch 27, sl st in 2nd ch from hook, sl st in each of next 2 chs, sc in each of next 4 chs, hdc in each of next 2 chs, hdc in each of next 12 chs, sc in each of next 4 chs, sl st in each of next 3 chs, turn. *(26 sts)*

Rows 2–10: Ch 1; working in **back lps** *(see Stitch Guide)* only, sl st in each of next 3 sts; working in both lps, sc in each of next 4 sts, hdc in each of next 12 sts, sc in each of next 4 sts; working in back lps only, sl st in each of next 3 sts, turn. At end of row 10, fasten off.

Row 11: Holding 2 Mitten Halves tog, matching sts and working through both thicknesses at once, join yarn with a sl st in first rem lp of foundation ch at base of row 1, sl st in each of next 26 sts, sl st evenly sp across ends of rows, sl st in each of first 23 sts across row 10, leave last 3 sl sts unworked. Fasten off.

Finishing

Weave 12-inch length of yarn through sl sts of row 11 at fingertips, pull gently to gather slightly. Fasten off.

Cut ribbon in half. Beg at center front, weave ribbon through sc sts just below 3 sl sts of cuff, tie ends in bow at center front. Sew rosebud directly below bow. Rep for 2nd Mitten.

Join yarn with sl st at center back cuff, ch 100, sl st at center back cuff on rem Mitten, turn, sl st in each ch across, sl st in edge of Mitten. Fasten off. ❑❑

Watercolors Blanket

Design by Glenda Winkleman

FINISHED SIZE
35 x 38 inches

MATERIALS
- ❑ Fine (sport) weight yarn (6 oz/480 yds/170g per skein):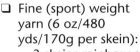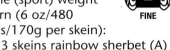
    - 3 skeins rainbow sherbet (A)
    - 1 skein each lavender (B) and light pink (C)
- ❑ Size H/8/5mm crochet hook or size needed to obtain gauge
- ❑ Yarn needle

GAUGE
4 hdc = 1 inch; 3 rows hdc = 1 inch

SPECIAL STITCH
Picot: Ch 3, sl st in last dc made.

INSTRUCTIONS

AFGHAN

Row 1: With A, ch 125, hdc in 2nd ch from hook, hdc in each rem ch across, turn. *(124 hdc)*

Row 2: Ch 1, hdc in first hdc, [sk next hdc, hdc in next hdc, hdc in sk hdc] across to last hdc, hdc in last hdc, turn.

Row 3: Ch 1, hdc in each hdc across, turn.

Rows 4–105: Rep rows 2 & 3 alternately. At end of row 105, do not fasten off. Do not turn.

Border

Rnd 1 (RS): Ch 1; [working over end sts of rows, work 105 hdc across to next corner, ch 2, work 124 hdc across to next corner, ch 2] twice, join with sl st in first hdc. Fasten off. Do not turn. *(458 hdc, 4 ch-2 sps)*

Rnd 2: Join B with a sl st in beg hdc, ch 1, hdc in same st as joining, [hdc in each hdc to next ch-2 sp, (2 hdc, ch 2, hdc) in ch-2 sp, hdc in each hdc to next ch-2 sp, (hdc, ch 2, 2 hdc) in ch-2 sp] twice, join with sl st in beg hdc. *(470 hdc, 4 ch-2 sps)*

Rnd 3: Ch 1, hdc in each hdc around, working (dc, ch 2, dc) in each ch-2 sp, join with sl st in beg hdc. *(478 sts, 4 ch-2 sps)*

Rnd 4: Ch 1, hdc in each st around, working 3 hdc in each ch-2 sp, join with sl st in beg hdc. Fasten off. Do not turn. *(490 hdc)*

Rnd 5: Join C with a sl st in beg hdc, ch 1, (sc, ch 1, sc) in same st as joining, sk next hdc, [(sc, ch 1, sc) in next hdc, sk next hdc] around, join with sl st in beg sc. Fasten off. Do not turn.

Rnd 6: Join B with a sl st in first ch-1 sp, (ch 3, dc, **picot**—*see Special Stitch*) in same st as joining, (2 dc, picot) in each ch-1 sp around, join with sl st in 3rd ch of beg ch-3. Fasten off. ❑❑

Pretty in Pink Preemie Afghan

Design by Cindy Carlson

SKILL LEVEL

INTERMEDIATE

FINISHED SIZE

15 x 16½ inches

MATERIALS

- ❑ Fine (baby) weight yarn (6 oz/447 yds/170g per skein):
    1 skein each shaded rose twinkle *(MC)* and white *(CC)*
- ❑ Size E/4/3.5mm crochet hook or size needed to obtain gauge
- ❑ Tapestry needle
- ❑ Bead needle
- ❑ White sewing thread
- ❑ 12-inch length ¼-inch-wide pink satin ribbon
- ❑ 3 (6mm) pearl beads
- ❑ Straight pins

GAUGE

6 sc = 1 inch; 6 sc rows = 1 inch

SPECIAL STITCHES

Small roll stitch (small roll st): Yo hook 7 times, insert hook in indicated st, yo, draw up a lp, yo, draw through all 9 lps on hook.

Large roll stitch (large roll st): Yo hook 12 times, insert hook in indicated st, yo, draw up a lp, yo, draw through all 14 lps on hook.

INSTRUCTIONS

AFGHAN

Row 1: With MC, ch 71, sc in 2nd ch from hook, dc in next ch, [sc in next ch, dc in next ch] across, turn. *(70 sts)*

Rows 2–56: Ch 1, [sc in next dc, dc in next sc] across, turn.

Rnd 57: Ch 1, [3 sc in corner st, sc in each st across to next corner, 3 sc in corner st; working over end sts of rows across, work 70 sc evenly sp across side to next corner] twice, join with sl st in beg sc. Fasten off.

Hood

Row 1: With CC, ch 2, 3 sc in 2nd ch from hook, turn. *(3 sc)*

Row 2: Ch 1, 2 sc in first sc, sc in next sc, 2 sc in last sc, turn. *(5 sc)*

Rows 3–26: Ch 1, 2 sc in first sc, sc in each sc across to last sc, 2 sc in last sc, turn. *(53 sc at end of row 26)*

At end of row 26, fasten off. Turn.

Row 27: Join MC with a sl st in first sc, ch 4 *(counts as first dc, ch-1)*, sk next st, [**small roll st** *(see Special*

Stitches) in next st, ch 1, sk next st] across to last st, dc in last st. Fasten off. Do not turn.

Row 28: Join MC with sl st in 3rd ch of beg ch-4, ch 1, sc in same st, sc in each ch-1 sp and roll st across, to last dc, sc in last dc. Fasten off.

Finishing

Place Hood at any corner of Afghan, matching corner sc of rnd 57 with opposite side of foundation ch at base of row 1 of Hood. Matching sts, pin Hood to Afghan.

Join Hood to Afghan:

Rnd 1: Working through both thicknesses, join CC with sl st at top corner of Hood, ch 1, 3 sc in same st, sc evenly spaced across to last row of Hood, sc in each sc of last rnd of Afghan, working 3 sc in each corner sc, around to opposite side of Hood, sc evenly spaced across Hood to beg sc, join with sl st in beg sc.

Rnd 2: Ch 1, sc in each sc around, working 3 sc in each corner sc, join with sl st in beg sc. Fasten off.

Flower

Make 3.

Rnd 1: With MC, ch 5, join with sl st to form ring, [ch 3, **large roll st** *(see Special Stitches)* in ring, sl st in ring] 5 times. Fasten off.

Thread bead needle with white sewing thread and sew pearl bead to center of any flower. With tapestry needle and yarn, using photo as a guide, sew Flower to Hood. Rep for 2 rem Flowers.

Cut ribbon in half and tie each section in bow. With sewing needle and thread, sew 1 bow to each bottom corner of Hood. ❑❑

There are no unwanted children, just unfound families.

—*The National Adoption Center*

Baby Booties

Design by Sue Childress

FINISHED SIZE
3 inches long

MATERIALS

- ❏ Fine (sport) weight crochet cotton (1¾ oz /202 yds/50g per ball):
  1 ball each light rose and yellow
- ❏ Size B/1/2.25mm crochet hook or size needed to obtain gauge
- ❏ 2 yds ⅛-inch-wide white satin ribbon
- ❏ Safety pin or other small marker

GAUGE
6 sc = 1 inch; 5 sc rows = 1 inch

SPECIAL STITCH
Treble crochet decrease (tr dec): Holding back last lp of each st on hook, tr in each of next 3 indicated sts, yo, draw through all 4 lps on hook.

INSTRUCTIONS
BOOTIE
Make 2 each light rose and yellow.
Sole
Rnd 1: Beg at heel, ch 15, 3 hdc in 3rd ch from hook, hdc in each of next 11 chs, 5 dc in last ch; working in rem lps across opposite side of foundation ch, hdc in each of next 11 chs, hdc in same ch as beg hdc, join with sl st in last ch of foundation ch. (32 sts, counting last 2 chs of foundation ch as first hdc)

Rnd 2: Ch 2 (counts as first hdc throughout), 2 hdc in next st, hdc in each of next 14 sts, 2 hdc in each of next 4 sts, hdc in each of next 12 sts, join with sl st in 2nd ch of beg ch-2. (37 hdc)

Rnd 3: Ch 2, hdc in each of next 18 hdc, 2 dc in each of next 5 hdc, hdc in each of next 13 hdc, join with sl st in 2nd ch of beg ch-2. (42 sts)

Rnd 4: Ch 1, 2 sc in same st as joining, 2 sc in each of next 2 sts, sc in each

of next 16 sts, 2 sc in each of next 7 sts, sc in each of next 13 sts, 2 sc in each of last 3 sts, join with sl st in beg sc. (55 sc)

Note: Do not join rem rnds unless otherwise specified. Mark first st of each rnd with safety pin or other small marker.

Rnd 5: Ch 1; working in **back lps** (see Stitch Guide) only, sc in same sc as joining, sc in each rem sc around.

Rnds 6–8: Sc in each sc around.

Rnd 9: Hdc in each of next 19 sc, [**tr dec** (see Special Stitch) in next 3 sc] 6 times, hdc in each of next 18 sc. (43 sts)

Rnd 10: Hdc in each of next 16 sts, [tr dec in next 3 sts] 4 times, hdc in each of next 15 sts. (35 sts)

Rnd 11: Hdc in each of next 16 sts, tr dec in next 3 sts, hdc in each of next 16 sts. (33 sts)

Rnd 12: [Sc in next st, ch 2] around, join with sl st in beg sc.

Cut ribbon into two 18-inch lengths. Beg at center front, weave one length of ribbon through sts of rnd 11 and tie in bow at front. Tie knot in each end of ribbon. Rep with rem ribbon on rem Bootie. ❏❏

Babies are such a nice way to start people.

—Don Herold

Few things are more delightful to observe than a child's limitless imagination at work in carefree, playtime fun. The cuddly stuffed animals, sweet baby doll and enchanting little playbooks included here are sure to delight all the lucky children who receive them.

Kitty & Puppy Neck Nuzzlers

Designs by Michele Wilcox

SKILL LEVEL

■ ■ ■ ▢ ▢

EASY

FINISHED SIZES

Kitty: 31 inches long
Puppy: 29 inches long

MATERIALS

- Red Heart Light & Lofty super bulky (super chunky) weight yarn (6 oz/140 yds/170g per skein): 2 skeins each onyx #9312 (A) and café au lait #9334 (B) 1 skein puff #9316 (C)
- Medium (worsted) weight yarn: 1 yd brown

6 SUPER BULKY

- Size 3 pearl crochet cotton: small amount each peach and blue
- Size P/Q/15mm crochet hook or size needed to obtain gauge
- Tapestry needle
- Sewing needle
- Sewing thread
- Polyester fiberfill
- 1 bag poly-pellets
- 1 pair each white and black panty hose
- Yarn marker

GAUGE

2 sc = 1 inch; 2 sc rnds = 1 inch

INSTRUCTIONS

Before beg to crochet, cut legs from panty hose, insert one leg into the other. Fill double nylon stocking with 16-oz pellets. Place pellet-filled stocking on flat surface and measure from tip to toe for 18 inches. Sew across this area to close opening. Cut off excess stocking.

KITTY

Head

Note: *Do not join rnds unless otherwise specified. Mark first st of each rnd with safety pin or other small marker.*

Rnd 1: With A, ch 2, 6 sc in 2nd ch from hook. *(6 sc)*

Rnd 2: [Sc in next sc, 2 sc in next sc] around. *(9 sc)*

Rnd 3: Sc in each sc around.

Rnd 4: 2 sc in each sc around. *(18 sc)*

Rnd 5: Rep rnd 3.

Rnd 6: [Sc in each of next 5 sc, 2 sc in next sc] around. *(21 sc)*

Rnds 7 & 8: Rep rnd 3. Stuff Head with polyester fiberfill.

Rnd 9: [Sc in next sc, **sc dec** *(see Stitch Guide)* in next 2 sc] around. *(14 sts)*

Rnd 10: [Sc dec in next 2 sts] around, join with sl st in beg sc dec. Leaving short length for finishing, fasten off. *(7 sts)*

With tapestry needle, weave length left for finishing through sts of last rnd, draw opening closed. Fasten off.

With tapestry needle and pearl cotton, using photo as a guide, embroider blue satin st eyes, peach satin st nose and peach straight st mouth.

Ear
Make 2.

Note: *Do not join rnds unless otherwise specified. Mark first st of each rnd with safety pin or other small marker.*

Rnd 1: With A, ch 2, 4 sc in 2nd ch from hook. *(4 sc)*

Rnd 2: 2 sc in each sc around. *(8 sc)*

Rnd 3: Sc in each sc around, join with sl st in beg sc. Leaving short length for finishing, fasten off.

Fold rnd 3 in half and sew opening closed with length left for finishing. Using photo as a guide, sew to top of Head.

Body
Note: *Do not join rnds unless otherwise specified. Mark first st of each rnd with safety pin or other small marker.*

Rnd 1: With A, ch 2, 6 sc in 2nd ch from hook. *(6 sc)*

Rnd 2: 2 sc in each sc around. *(12 sc)*

Rnd 3: [Sc in next sc, 2 sc in next sc] around. *(18 sc)*

Rnds 4–36: Sc in each sc around. At end of rnd 36, insert panty hose pellet bag.

Rnd 37: [Sc in next sc, sc dec in next 2 sc] around. *(12 sts)*

Rnd 38: [Sc dec in next 2 sts] around, join with sl st in beg sc. Leaving short length for finishing, fasten off. With tapestry needle, weave length left for finishing through sts of last rnd, draw opening closed, fasten off.

Sew Head to top edge of Body over rnds 3–5.

Leg
Note: *Do not join rnds unless otherwise specified. Mark first st of each rnd with safety pin or other small marker.*

Make 2 legs with A only.

Make 2 legs with rnds 1–4 in C and rnds 4–12 in A.

Rnd 1: Ch 2, 6 sc in 2nd ch from hook. *(6 sc)*

Rnd 2: 2 sc in each sc around. *(12 sc)*

Rnds 3 & 4: Sc in each sc around.

Rnd 5: [Sc dec in next 2 sc] around. *(6 sc)*

Rnds 6–12: Sc in each st around. At end of rnd 12, join with sl st in beg sc. Leaving short length for finishing, fasten off.

Do not stuff Legs. With tapestry needle and lengths left for finishing, sew 2 Legs to each side of Body.

Tail
Note: *Do not join rnds unless otherwise specified. Mark first st of each rnd with safety pin or other small marker.*

Rnd 1: With C, ch 2, 6 sc in 2nd ch from hook. *(6 sc)*

Rnds 2–6: Sc in each sc around. At end of rnd 6, join with sl st in beg sc. Fasten off.

Rnd 7: Join A with sl st in beg sc, ch

1; sc in same st as joining, sc in each rem sc around.

Rnds 8–12: Sc in each sc around. At end of rnd 12, join with sl st in beg sc. Fasten off, leaving short length for finishing.

Do not stuff Tail. With tapestry needle and length left for finishing, sew tail to back Body slightly above back Legs.

PUPPY
Head
Note: *Do not join rnds unless otherwise specified. Mark first st of each rnd with safety pin or other small Marker.*

Rnd 1: With B, ch 2, 6 sc in 2nd ch from hook. *(6 sc)*

Rnd 2: Sc in each sc around.

Rnd 3: [Sc in next sc, 2 sc in next sc] around. *(9 sc)*

Rnd 4: [2 sc in next sc] 6 times, sc in each of next 3 sc, mark last 3 sc made for bottom of Head. *(15 sc)*

Rnd 5: Rep rnd 2.

Rnd 6: [Sc in next sc, 2 sc in next sc] 6 times, sc in each of next 3 sc. *(21 sc)*

Rnds 7–10: Rep rnd 2.

Rnd 11: [Sc in next sc, sc dec in next 2 sc] around. *(14 sts)*.

Stuff head with polyester fiberfill.

Rnd 12: [Sc dec in next 2 sts] around, join with sl st in beg sc dec. Leaving short length for finishing, fasten off. With tapestry needle, weave length for finishing through sts of last rnd,

> *Because they are children, and for no other reason, they have dignity and worth simply because they are.*
>
> —*Unknown*

draw opening closed, Fasten off. With tapestry needle and brown yarn, embroider satin st eyes and nose, straight st mouth.

Ear
Make 2.
Rnds 1–3: Rep rnds 1–3 of Head.
Rnds 4–6: Sc in each sc around.
Rnd 7: [Sc in next sc, sc dec in next 2 sc] around, join with sl st in beg sc dec. Leaving short length for finishing, fasten off. Fold rnd 7 in half. With length left for finishing, sew opening closed. Sew Ear to side of Head.

Body
Rnds 1–38: With B, rep rnds 1–38 of Kitty Body.

Leg
Note: *Do not join rnds unless otherwise specified. Mark first st of each rnd with safety pin or other small marker.*
Make 4.
Rnd 1: With B, ch 2, 6 sc in 2nd ch from hook. *(6 sc)*
Rnd 2: 2 sc in each sc around. *(12 sc)*
Rnds 3 & 4: Sc in each sc around.
Rnd 5: [Sc dec in next 2 sc] around. *(6 sts)*
Rnds 6–12: Sc in each st around. At end of rnd 12, join with sl st in beg sc. Leaving short length for finishing, fasten off.
Do not stuff Leg. With tapestry needle and length left for finishing, sew opening closed. Sew 2 Legs to each end of Body.

Tail
Note: *Do not join rnds unless otherwise specified. Mark first st of each rnd with safety pin or other small marker.*
Rnd 1: With B, ch 2, 6 sc in 2nd ch from hook. *(6 sc)*
Rnds 2–11: Sc in each sc around. At end of rnd 11, join with sl st in beg sc. Leaving short length for finishing, fasten off.
Do not stuff Tail. With tapestry needle and length left for finishing, sew opening closed. Sew Tail to Body slightly above hind Legs. ❏❏

Sweetie Pie Baby

Design by Kathleen Stuart

SKILL LEVEL
■□□□
BEGINNER

FINISHED SIZE
11 inches long

MATERIALS
❏ Fine (sport) weight yarn:
  2 oz/200 yds/57g pink
  1 oz/100 yds/28g each off-white, light yellow, red and light brown
❏ Size G/6/4mm crochet hook or size needed to obtain gauge
❏ Tapestry needle
❏ Polyester fiberfill
❏ Stitch Marker

2 FINE

GAUGE
5 sc = 1 inch

PATTERN NOTES
To change color in single crochet decrease, work last single crochet decrease before color change as follows: [insert hook in next stitch, yarn over with working color, draw up a loop] twice, drop working color to wrong side, yarn over with next color, draw through all 3 loops on hook. To change color in double crochet, work last double crochet before color change until last 2 loops before final yarn over remain on hook, drop working color to wrong side, yarn over with next color, complete double crochet.

INSTRUCTIONS
DOLL
Head
Note: *Do not join rnds unless otherwise specified. Mark first st of each rnd with safety pin or other small marker.*
Rnd 1 (RS): Beg at top of head, with off-white, ch 2, 6 sc in 2nd ch from hook. *(6 sc)*
Rnd 2: 2 sc in each sc around. *(12 sc)*
Rnd 3: [Sc in next sc, 2 sc in next sc] around. *(18 sc)*
Rnd 4: [Sc in each of next 2 sc, 2 sc in next sc] around. *(24 sc)*
Rnd 5: [Sc in each of next 3 sc, 2 sc in next sc] around. *(30 sc)*
Rnd 6: [Sc in each of next 4 sc, 2 sc in next sc] around. *(36 sc)*
Rnds 7–12: Sc in each sc around.
Rnd 13: [Sc in each of next 4 sc, **sc dec** *(see Stitch Guide)* in next 2 sc] around. *(30 sts)*
Rnd 14: [Sc in each of next 3 sts, sc dec in next 2 sts] around. *(24 sts)*
Rnd 15: [Sc in each of next 2 sts, sc dec in next 2 sts] around. Do not fasten off. *(18 sts)*
Stuff Head with polyester fiberfill.

Body
Rnd 16: [Sc in next st, sc dec in next 2 sts] around, changing to pink in last st.. *(12 sts)*
Rnds 17 & 18: Rep rnds 3 and 4. *(24 sc at end of rnd 18)*
Rnd 19: [Dc in each of next 3 sc, 2 dc in next sc] around. *(30 dc)*
Rnd 20: [Dc in each of next 4 dc, 2 dc in next dc] around. *(36 dc)*
Rnds 21–29: Dc in each dc around. At end of rnd 29, do not fasten off.
Stuff Body with polyester fiberfill.

First Leg
Rnd 1: Dc in each of first 9 dc, sk 18 dc, dc in each of last 9 dc. *(18 dc)*
Rnds 2–8: Dc in each dc around.
Rnd 9: [Dc in next dc, **dc dec** *(see Stitch Guide)* in next 2 dc] around. *(12 sts)*
Rnd 10: [Dc dec in next 2 dc] 6 times, join with sl st in beg dc. Fasten off, leaving short length for finishing.
Stuff First Leg with polyester fiberfill. With tapestry needle and length left for finishing, sew First Leg opening closed.

2nd Leg

Rnd 1: Join pink with sl st in next unworked dc of rnd 29 of Body, ch 3 (counts as first dc), dc in each of next 17 dc. (18 dc)

Rnds 2–10: Rep rnds 2–10 of First Leg.

With tapestry needle and pink, sew crotch opening closed.

Arm

Make 2.

Note: Do not join rnds unless otherwise specified. Mark first st of each rnd with safety pin or other small marker.

Rnd 1: With pink, ch 2, 6 sc in 2nd ch from hook. (6 sc)

Rnd 2: 2 dc in each sc around. (12 dc)

Rnds 3–9: Dc in each dc around, changing to off-white in last dc of rnd 9.

Stuff Arm with polyester fiberfill as work progresses.

Rnds 10 & 11: Dc in each dc around.

Rnd 12: [Dc dec in next 2 dc] around, join with sl st in beg dc. Leaving short length for finishing, fasten off.

Finish stuffing Arm. With length left for finishing, sew hand opening closed. Sew Arm to side of Body over rnds 17–19.

Bonnet

Rnds 1–6: With pink, rep rnds 1–6 of Head. (36 sc at end of rnd 6)

Rnd 7: [Sc in each of next 5 sc, 2 sc in next sc] around. (42 sc)

Rnd 8: [Sc in each of next 6 sc, 2 sc in next sc] around. (48 sc)

Rnd 9: [Sc in each of next 7 sc, 2 sc in next sc] around. (54 sc)

Rnd 10: [Sc in each of next 8 sc, 2 sc in next sc] around. (60 sc)

Row 11: Working in **back lps** (see Stitch Guide) only, 2 dc in each of next 49 sc, (dc, ch 3, sl st) in next sc, leaving rem sts unworked. Fasten off.

Finishing

Using photo as a guide, embroider V-shapes for eyes over rnd 8 of

Head with tapestry needle and light brown, leaving 2 sc free between eyes. With red, embroider mouth centered below eyes over rnds 11 and 12 of Head.

For hair, wrap light yellow several times around 2 fingers held tog, remove lps from fingers and tack to center front of Head over rnd 2.

Weave 10-inch length of pink yarn through base of dc sts of row 11 of Bonnet, leaving equal length extending from each end. Placed Bonnet on Head, pull ends gently and double-knot under chin. Tie ends in a bow and trim ends evenly. With tapestry needle and pink, tack Bonnet to Head. ❑❑

Fun-Time Play Books

Designs by Karen Isak

SKILL LEVEL

EASY

FINISHED SIZE

5 inches square

MATERIALS

- Medium (worsted) weight yarn:
  2 oz/100 yds 57g each turquoise, yellow and brown
  1 oz/28g/50 yd each red, white, pink and green
- 6-strand embroidery floss: 1 skein each black, red and white
- Size G/6/4mm crochet hook or size needed to obtain gauge
- Tapestry needle
- Yarn needle
- Polyester fiberfill
- 3 story books, each 3¼ x 2¾ inches

GAUGE

7 sc = 2 inches; 4 sc rows = 1 inch

INSTRUCTIONS

FISH BOOK
Book Cover
Make 2.

Row 1: With turquoise, ch 17, sc in 2nd ch from hook, sc in each rem ch across, turn. *(16 sc)*

Rows 2–11: Ch 1, sc in each sc across, turn.

Row 12: Ch 1, **sc dec** (see Stitch Guide) in first 2 sc, sc in each sc across to last 2 sc, sc dec in last 2 sc, turn. *(14 sts)*

Rows 13–18: Rep row 12. *(2 sts at end of row 18)*

Row 19: Ch 1, sc dec in next 2 sts. Do not turn. *(1 st)*

Rnd 20: Ch 1, sc evenly sp around entire Book, join with sl st in **back lp** (see Stitch Guide) only of beg sc. Do not turn.

Rnd 21: Ch 1; beg in same st as joining, working in back lps only, sc in each sc around, join with sl st in beg sc, do not turn.

Rnd 22: Ch 1; beg in same st as joining, sc in each sc around, join with sl st in back lp only of beg sc, do not turn.

Rnds 23–26: Rep rnds 21 and 22 alternately. At end of rnd 26, fasten off, leaving length for finishing.

With yarn needle and length left for finishing, sew rnd 26 to inside of piece, forming a ridge and stuffing with polyester fiberfill as work progresses.

Holding 2 sections together, using photo as a guide, sew seam from bottom upward for 10 sts. Cut 2 lengths of turquoise and attach to each edge of Book opening on opposite side from seam. To close Book, tie ends in a bow.

Wave
Row 1: With white, ch 15, sc in 2nd ch from hook, *ch 6, sl st in 2nd ch from hook, [sc dec in next 2 chs] twice**, sc in each of next 3 chs of ch-16, rep from * across, ending last rep at **, sl st in last ch. Fasten off, leaving short length for finishing. With yarn needle, sew Wave to front of Book Cover.

Fish
Make 3.

Row 1: With yellow, ch 2, 2 sc in 2nd ch from hook, turn. *(2 sc)*

Row 2: Ch 1, 2 sc in first sc, sc in next sc, turn. *(3 sc)*

Row 3: Ch 1, sc in first sc, 2 sc in next sc, sc in next sc, turn. *(4 sc)*

Rows 4–6: Ch 1, sc in each sc across, turn.

Row 7: Ch 1, [sc dec in next 2 sc] twice, turn. *(2 sts)*

Row 8: Ch 1, sc dec in next 2 sts. *(1 st)*

Rnd 9: Sl st over end st of each row down to row 1, sl st in rem lp of ch at base of row 1, sl st over end st of each row to row 8, join with sl st in beg sl st. Fasten off.

With tapestry needle and black embroidery floss, using photo as a guide, embroider mouth and gills with straight st on 2 Fishes. Make eye of French knot with black embroidery floss.

Joining 2 Embroidered Fishes
Rnd 10: Working through both thicknesses in back lps only of rnd 9 sl sts, join pink with a sl st over last st of row 8, (sc, 2 dc, sc) in same st, sl st around to last st before beg sc, (sc, 2 dc, sc) in last st, join with sl st in beg sc. Fasten off.

With yellow, leaving short length for finishing, ch 12. Fasten off, leaving short length for finishing. With yarn needle and lengths left for finishing, using photo as a guide, sew ch-12 vertically to inside back of Book Cover. Tuck embroidered Fish under ch.

3rd Fish
Rnd 10: Join pink with a sl st over last st of row 8, rep rnd 10 for Joining 2 Embroidered Fishes. Fasten off, leaving short length for finishing.

With yarn needle and length left for finishing, sew 3rd Fish to front of Book Cover.

Book Holder
Row 1: With turquoise, ch 20 dc in 5th ch from hook, [ch 2, sk next 2 chs, dc in next ch] across, turn.

Row 2: Ch 5 *(counts as first dc, ch-2)*, dc in next dc, [ch 2, dc in next dc] across, ending with ch 2, sk 2 chs, dc in next ch of foundation ch.

Row 3: Rep row 2. Fasten off, leaving length for finishing..

With yarn needle and length left for finishing, using photo as a guide, sew Book Holder to inside front section of Book Cover.

FLOWER BOOK
Book Cover
Make 2.

Row 1–Rnd 26: With yellow, rep row 1–rnd 26 of Book Cover for Fish Book.

Finish as for Book Cover for Fish Book.

Fence
Make 2.

Row 1: With white, ch 4, 2 sc in 2nd ch from hook, sc in each of next 2 chs, turn. *(4 sc)*

Row 2: Ch 1, sc in each of next 3 sc, turn. *(3 sc)*

Row 3: Ch 1, 2 sc in first sc, sc in each of next 2 sc, turn. *(4 sc)*

Rows 4–15: Rep rows 2 and 3 alternately. At end of row 15, do not turn.

Row 16: Ch 1; sc over end st of each row across to row 1, ch 1, sc in rem lp of each of next 3 chs of foundation ch at base of row 1. Fasten off, leaving short length for finishing.

With yarn needle and length left for finishing, sew 1 Fence to front of Book Cover. Sew rem Fence to inside front section of Book Cover to serve as Book Holder.

Book Cover Flower
Stem
With green, ch 12. Leaving short length for finishing, fasten off.

With yarn needle and length left for finishing, sew stem to bottom front of Book Cover with bottom edge just below top edge of Fence.

Leaves
With green, ch 8. Leaving short length for finishing, fasten off.

With yarn needle and length left for finishing, using photo as a guide, place center of ch-8 directly over Stem and sew in place in V-shape.

Flower
Rnd 1: With white, ch 2, 7 sc in 2nd ch from hook, join with sl st in beg sc. Fasten off. *(7 sc)*

Rnd 2: Join red with sl st in any sc, ch 3, [sl st in next sc, ch 3] around, join with sl st in beg sl st. Fasten off.

With tapestry needle and black embroidery floss, using photo as a guide, embroider eyes and mouth over rnd 1. Sew Flower to Book Cover at top of Stem.

Flower Baby
Stem
Rnd 1: With green, ch 2, 7 sc in 2nd ch from hook, join with sl st in beg sc, turn.

Rnds 2–8: Ch 1, sc in each sc around, join with sl st in beg sc. At end of rnd 8, fasten off, leaving short length for finishing. Fasten off.

Leaf
Join green with sl st over any sc of rnd 5, *ch 1, 2 sc in same st. Fasten off.* Join green with sl st over sc of rnd 5 on opposite side of Stem, rep between *.

Stuff Stem with polyester fiberfill. With yarn needle and length left for finishing, sew top of Stem closed.

Flower Center
Make 2.
Rnd 1: With white, ch 2, 7 sc in 2nd ch from hook, join with sl st in beg sc. *(7 sc)*

Rnd 2: Ch 1, 2 sc in each sc around, join with sl st in beg sc. Fasten off. *(14 sc)*

With tapestry needle and black embroider floss, embroider eyes and mouth on 1 Flower.

Flower Petals
Holding 2 Flower Centers tog and working through both thicknesses at once, join red with a sl st in any sc on last rnd, ch 1, 2 sc in same sc, (sl st, 2 sc) in each sc around, join with sl st in beg sl st. Fasten off, leaving short length for finishing.

With yarn needle and length left for

finishing, sew Flower to top of Stem. With green, leaving short length for finishing, ch 12. Fasten off, leaving short length for finishing. With yarn needle and lengths left for finishing, using photo as a guide, sew ch-12 horizontally to inside back of Book Cover. Tuck Flower Baby under ch.

GINGERBREAD BOOK
Book Cover
Make 2.
Row 1–Rnd 26: With brown, rep row 1–rnd 26 of Book Cover for Fish Book.

Finish as for Book Cover for Fish Book.

Candy Cane
Make 2.
Holding one strand each red and white tog, ch 15. Fasten off.

With yarn needle and yarn, using photo as a guide, sew Candy Canes to outside front of Book Cover, shaping top of Candy Canes and crossing at center.

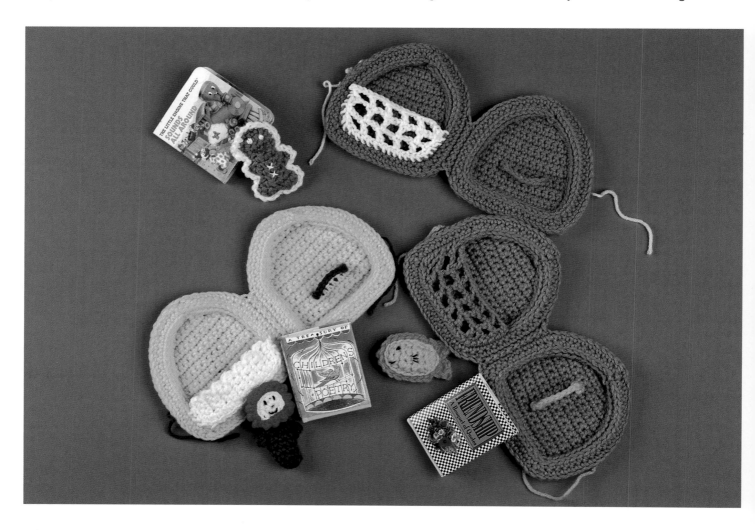

Icing

Join white with sl st over **post** (see Stitch Guide) of sc at end of row 12 at top of Book Cover, ch 1, sc in same st; working evenly sp across top of Book Cover to corresponding st on opposite side of row 12, [ch 2, sc over post of st on Book Cover] across. Fasten off.

Gingerbread Doll
Make 2.

Row 1: Beg at top of Head with brown, ch 5, sc in 2nd ch from hook, sc in each rem ch across, turn. (4 sc)

Row 2: Ch 1, 2 sc in first sc, sc in each sc across to last sc, 2 sc in last sc, turn. (6 sc)

Row 3: Ch 1, sc in each sc across, turn.

Row 4: Ch 1, [sc dec in next 2 sts] 3 times, turn. (3 sts)

Row 5: Ch 1, sc in each st across, turn.

Row 6: Ch 1, 2 sc in first sc, sc in next sc, 2 sc in last sc, turn. (5 sc)

Row 7: Rep row 2. (7 sc)

Row 8: Ch 1, sl st in each of first 2 sc, (sl st, ch 1, sc) in next sc, sc in each of next 2 sc, turn. (3 sc)

Row 9: Rep row 6.

Row 10: Ch 1, (sc, dc) in first sc, (dc, sc) in next sc, sl st in next sc, (sc, dc) in next sc, (dc, sc, sl st) in last sc. Fasten off.

On 1 piece, with tapestry needle and embroidery floss, using photo as a guide, embroider eyes and 2 cross-stitch buttons with white. Embroider mouth with red.

Join 2 Gingerbread Dolls

Holding 2 Dolls tog, working through both thicknesses and stuffing with polyester fiberfill as work progresses, join white with sl st at top of Doll, sl st around, join with sl st in beg sl st. Fasten off.

With brown, leaving short length for finishing, ch 12. Fasten off, leaving short length for finishing. With yarn needle and lengths left for finishing, using photo as a guide, sew ch-12 horizontally to inside back of Book Cover. Tuck Gingerbread Doll under ch.

Book Holder

Rows 1–3: With white, rep rows 1–3 of Book Holder for Fish Book.

With yarn needle and length left for finishing, using photo as a guide, sew Book Holder to inside front section of Book Cover. ❏❏

For the wonderful furry friends who enrich our lives, these pet-pleasing projects are the perfect accessories for the loving and loyal pets that steal our hearts and ask no more of us than good care and the pleasures of being loved.

Woven Jewels Blankie

Design by Belinda "Bendy" Carter

SKILL LEVEL

EASY

FINISHED SIZE

24 inches square

MATERIALS

- ❏ Red Heart Super Saver medium (worsted) weight yarn (Solids: 7 oz/364 yds/198g per skein; Multis: 5 oz/278 yds/141g per skein):

  MEDIUM 4

  His:
  2 skeins each fiesta jewel print #399 *(MC)* and black #312 *(CC)*

Hers:
2 skeins each Monet print #310 *(MC)* and white #311 *(CC)*

- ❏ Sizes F/5/3.75mm and G/6/4mm crochets or size needed to obtain gauge
- ❏ Yarn needle

We call them dumb animals, and so they are, for they cannot tell us how they feel, but they do not suffer less because they have not words.

—Anna Sewell

GAUGE

Size G hook and 1 strand MC worked over 3 strands CC held tog: 17 sc = 4 inches

PATTERN NOTE

Wind CC into 3 equal balls before beginning.

INSTRUCTIONS

BLANKIE

Row 1 (RS): With size G hook and MC, ch 101; holding 3 strands of CC tog and working over them into ch sts with MC, sc in 2nd ch from hook, [ch 2, sk 2 chs, sc in next ch] across, turn. *(33 ch-2 sps)*

Row 2: Ch 1 around CC, lay CC over last row; working over CC with MC, sc in first sc, [ch 2, sc in next sc] across, turn.

Rep row 2 until Blankie measures 23½ inches from beg, ending with a WS row. At end of last row, fasten off CC only. Turn.

Edging

Rnd 1 (RS): With size F hook, ch 1, work 100 sc evenly sp across each side, working (sc, ch 2, sc) at each corner, join with sl st in beg sc.

Rnd 2: Ch 1; sc in same sc as joining, sc in each rem sc around, working (sc, ch 2, sc) in each corner ch-2 sp, join with sl st in beg sc. Fasten off. ❑❑

Braided-Look Pet Rug

Design by Darlene Polachic

SKILL LEVEL

BEGINNER

FINISHED SIZE

14½ x 19½ inches

MATERIALS

- ❑ Medium (worsted) weight yarn: 1¾ oz/88 yds/50g each of 7 colors as desired
- ❑ Size C/2/2.75mm crochet hook or size needed to obtain gauge
- ❑ Yarn needle

GAUGE

5 dc = 1 inch; 4 dc rnds = 1½ inches

PATTERN NOTES

Weave in loose ends as work progresses.

With additional materials, rug can be enlarged to any size desired by maintaining inc of 6 dc on each rounded end of rug.

INSTRUCTIONS

Rug

Row 1 (RS): With first color, ch 16, dc in 4th ch from hook, dc in each rem ch across, turn. Fasten off. *(14 dc, counting last 3 chs of foundation ch as first dc)*

Rnd 2: With RS facing, join next color with sl st in top of first dc, ch 3 *(counts as first dc throughout)*, dc in each dc across to last dc, 6 dc over side of last dc; working in rem lps of foundation ch, dc in each dc across, ending with 6 dc over side of first dc of row 1, join with sl st in 3rd ch of beg ch-3. *(36 dc)*

Rnd 3: Ch 3, dc in each rem dc around, working 2 dc in each of 6 dc sts at each rounded end of Rug, join with sl st in 3rd ch of beg ch-3. Fasten off. *(48 dc)*

Rnd 4: With RS facing, join next color with sl st in any dc, ch 3, dc in each dc around, working [2 dc in next dc, dc in next dc] 6 times on each rounded end of Rug, join with sl st in 3rd ch of beg ch-3. *(60 dc)*

Rnd 5: Ch 3, dc in each dc around, working [2 dc in next dc, dc in next dc] 6 times on each round end of Rug, join with sl st in 3rd ch of beg ch-3. *(72 dc)*

Rnd 6: Rep rnd 5. Fasten off. *(84 dc)*

Rnd 7: With RS facing, join next color with sl st in any dc, ch 3, dc in each dc around, working [2 dc in next dc, dc in each of next 2 dc] 6 times over 18 dc of each rounded end of Rug, join in 3rd ch of beg ch-3. *(96 dc)*

Rnd 8: Ch 3, dc in each dc around, working [2 dc in next dc, dc in each of next 3 dc] 6 times over 24 dc at each rounded end of Rug, join in 3rd ch of beg ch-3. *(108 dc)*

Rnd 9: Ch 3, dc in each dc around, working [2 dc in next dc, dc in each of next 4 dc] 6 times over 30 dc at each rounded end of Rug, join in 3rd ch of beg ch-3. *(120 dc)*

Rnds 10–18: Continuing in established pattern of 3 rnds of each color, ch 3, dc in each dc around, working [2 dc in next dc, dc in each of next 4 dc] 6 times over 30 dc at each rounded end of Rug, join with sl st in 3rd ch of beg ch-3. *(228 dc at end of rnd 18)*

Rnd 19: Join next color with sl st in any dc, ch 3, dc in each dc around, working [2 dc in next dc, dc in each of next 9 dc] 6 times over 60 dc at each rounded end of Rug, join with sl st in 3rd ch of beg ch-3. *(240 dc)*

Rnd 20: Rep rnd 19. Fasten off. *(252 dc)* ❑❑

They say the test of literary power is whether a man can write an inscription. I say, "Can he name a kitten?"

—Samuel Butler

Today's seniors are younger than ever and lead active lives enjoying a variety of hobbies, volunteering in their communities and even beginning second careers. You'll love stitching these cozy comforts especially chosen to sooth and pamper the special seniors in your life!

Warm & Soothing Heat Pack

Design by Ruthie Marks

SKILL LEVEL

EASY

FINISHED SIZE
10 x 15 inches

MATERIALS

- ❑ Brown Sheep Lambs Pride Superwash wool medium (worsted) weight yarn (3½ oz/200 yds/99.4g per skein):
    - 2 skeins sea foam #SW16 *(MC)*
    - 1 skein Emerald City #SW52 *(CC)*
- ❑ Size E/4/3.5mm crochet hook or size needed to obtain gauge
- ❑ Yarn needle
- ❑ Sewing needle
- ❑ Sewing thread
- ❑ 9 inch x 24½ inch piece of untreated cotton fabric
- ❑ Uncooked rice kernels

GAUGE
(Sc, hdc) 4 times = 1½ inches; 4 pattern rows = 1½ inches

INSTRUCTIONS

HEAT PACK
Body
Make 2.

Row 1: With MC, ch 43, sc in 2nd ch from hook, [(sc, hdc) in next ch, sk next ch] across, sc in last ch, turn. *(42 sts)*

Row 2: Ch 1; working in **front lps** *(see Stitch Guide)* only, sc in first sc, (sc, hdc) in each hdc across to last sc, sc in last sc, turn.

Rows 3–34: Rep row 2. At end of row 34, fasten off. Turn.

> *The greatest comfort of my old age, and that which gives me the highest satisfaction, is the pleasing remembrance of the many benefits I have done to others.*
>
> —*Cato the Elder*

Neck

Row 1: Sk first 14 sts of row 34, join MC with sl st in next sc, ch 1, sc in same sc, [(sc, hdc) in next hdc] 6 times, sk next sc, sc in next hdc, turn. *(14 sts)*

Rows 2–5: Rep row 2 of Body. At end of row 5, do not fasten off. Turn.

Edging

Ch 1, 3 sc in corner st, sc in each st across to last st of row 5, 3 sc in last st; **working over end sts of rows across side of Neck, work 4 sc evenly spaced to end of Neck**, **sc dec** *(see Stitch Guide)* in 2 sts at inner corner, sc in each rem st across row 34 of Body to last st, 3 sc in last st; *working over end sts of rows across side of Body, work 47 sc evenly spaced to next corner, 3 sc in corner st*; sc in each rem lp across foundation ch to next corner, 3 sc in corner st, rep from * to *, sc in each rem st across to 34 to inner corner, sc dec in 2 sts at inner corner, rep from ** to **, join with sl st in beg sc. Fasten off.

Bottom Trim

Row 1 (RS): Working across bottom edge, join CC with a sl st in first sc after 3 corner sc, ch 1, sc in same sc, sc in each sc across to last sc before next 3-sc corner group, turn.

Row 2: Ch 4 *(counts as first dc, ch 1)*, sk next sc, dc in next sc, [ch 1, sk next sc, dc in next sc] across. Fasten off.

Joining 2 Body Pieces

Row 1: Holding Body pieces with WS tog and working through both thicknesses across first long side toward Neck, join CC with sl st in first sc of 3-sc corner group at bottom right corner, ch 1, sc in same sc, 3 sc in corner sc, sc in each sc across to opposite bottom corner, working 3 sc in each corner sc and sc dec in 2 sc at each Neck edge inner corner, ending with 3 sc in corner sc at opposite bottom corner, sc in next sc, turn.

Row 2: Ch 3 *(counts as first dc)*, sl st back over edge of end st of row 2 of Bottom Trim, ch 2, [dc in next sc on last row, ch 2] 3 times, sk next sc, dc in next sc, [ch 1, sk next sc, dc in next sc] across to corresponding st at opposite bottom corner, adjusting number of sts skipped, if necessary, to work [ch 2, dc in first sc of 3-sc corner group, {ch 2, dc in next sc} twice, ch 2, sk next sc, dc in next sc] at each 3-sc corner group, ending with dc in last sc at opposite bottom corner, ch 2, sl st over end of row 1 of Bottom Trim. Fasten off.

Weaving Chain

With 2 strands of CC held tog, work ch 55 inches long. Fasten off.

Cotton Inner Bag

Fold untreated cotton fabric in half with RS tog to form 9 inch x 12¼ inch piece. With sewing needle and thread, sew ¼-inch seam across 1 long and 1 short edge. Turn Bag RS out. Reinforce edge by sewing across sewn edge again. Place uncooked rice kernels in Bag, turn edges of opening under ¼ inch and sew opening closed. Fold Bag in half so that each half contains ½ of rice kernels. With sewing needle and thread, sew across center of Bag to make 2 pockets of rice.

Finishing

Insert Cotton Inner Bag into Body. Beg at center of Bottom Trim, weave Weaving Chain through ch sps around. Tie ends in bow.

For warm therapy, place Pack in microwave and heat on high for 30-second intervals until desired temperature.

For cool temperature, place Pack in a plastic bag in the freezer and chill until desired temperature. ❑❑

Beddy-Bye Booties

Design by Sharon Phillips

SKILL LEVEL

EASY

FINISHED SIZE

One size fits most

MATERIALS

- ❑ Lion Brand Wool Ease medium (worsted) weight yarn (3 oz/197 yds/85g per ball): 1 ball rose heather #140

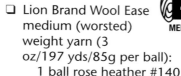

- ❑ Size I/9/5.5mm crochet hook or size needed to obtain gauge
- ❑ Sewing needle
- ❑ Sewing thread
- ❑ 18-inch length ½-inch-wide satin ribbon

GAUGE
4 dc = 1 inch; 2 dc rnds = 1 inch

INSTRUCTIONS
BOOTIE
Foot
Make 2.
Rnd 1: Beg at toe, ch 4, 11 dc in 4th ch from hook, join in 4th ch of beg ch-4. *(12 dc, counting last 3 chs of ch-4 as first dc)*

Rnd 2: Ch 3 *(counts as first dc throughout)*, dc in same dc as joining, 2 dc in each rem dc around, join with sl st in 3rd ch of beg ch-3. *(24 dc)*

Rnd 3: Ch 3, dc in same dc as joining, dc in each of next 3 dc, [2 dc in next dc, dc in each of next 3 dc] around, join with sl st in 3rd ch of beg ch-3. *(30 dc)*

Rnd 4: Ch 3, dc in each dc around, join with sl st in 3rd ch of beg ch-3.

Rep rnd 4 until desired length to heel. Do not fasten off at end of last rnd.

Heel
Rnd 1: Ch 3, dc in same dc as joining, dc in next dc, *[2 dc in next dc, dc in next dc] 3 times*, hdc in each of next 5 dc, sc in each of next 5 dc, hdc in each of next 5 dc, rep bet *, 2 dc in next dc, join with sl st in 3rd ch of beg ch-3. *(38 sts)*

Rnds 2–7: Ch 3, dc in each of next 11 sts, hdc in each of next 5 sts, sc in each of next 5 sts, hdc in each of next 5 sts, dc in each of next 11 sts, join with sl st in 3rd ch of beg ch-3.

Rnd 8: Ch 3, *dc dec *(see Stitch Guide)* in next 2 sts, [dc in next st, dc dec in next 2 sts] 3 times*, hdc in each of next 5 sts, sc in each of next 5 sts, hdc in each of next 5 sts, rep between *, join with sl st in 3rd ch of beg ch-3. Do not fasten off. *(30 sts)*

Cuff
Rnd 1: Ch 3, dc in each st around, join with sl st in 3rd ch of beg ch-3.

Rnd 2: Ch 3, **fpdc** *(see Stitch Guide)* around post of next dc, [**bpdc** *(see Stitch Guide)* around post of next dc, fpdc around post of next dc] around, join with sl st in 3rd ch of beg ch-3.

Rnds 3–8: Ch 3, fpdc around post of next sc, [bpdc around post of next st, fpdc around post of next st] around, join with sl st in 3rd ch of beg ch-3. At end of row 8, fasten off.

Cut 18-inch length of ribbon in half. Tie each half into bow. With sewing needle and thread, tack each bow to front of each Bootie at base of rnd 1 of Cuff. ❏❏

Many Textures Tote

Design by Cindy Carlson

SKILL LEVEL

EASY

FINISHED SIZE
9½ x 10½ inches, excluding Strap

MATERIALS
- ❑ Medium (worsted) weight yarn: 14 oz/700 yds/ 397g variegated
- ❑ Size G/6/4mm crochet hook or size needed to obtain gauge
- ❑ Yarn needle
- ❑ Sewing needle
- ❑ Sewing thread
- ❑ 1-inch brass key ring
- ❑ 2 decorative ⅞-inch buttons for tote
- ❑ Decorative ⅞-inch button for purse
- ❑ 1-inch length hook and loop fastening tape

GAUGE
7 sc = 2 inches; 8 sc rows = 2 inches

INSTRUCTIONS

TOTE
Front
Row 1: Beg at top edge, ch 35, sc in 2nd ch from hook, dc in next ch, [sc in next ch, dc in next ch] across, turn. *(34 sts)*

Rows 2–11: Ch 1, sc in each dc and dc in each sc across, turn.

Rows 12–31: Ch 1, sc in each st across, turn. At end of Row 31, fasten off.

Back
Row 1: Rep row 1 of Front.

Rows 2–24: Rep row 2 of Front. At end of row 24, fasten off.

Side
Make 2.
Row 1: Ch 9, sc in 2nd ch from hook, sc in each ch across, turn. *(8 sc)*

Rows 2–31: Ch 1, sc in each sc across, turn. At end of row 31, fasten off.

Bottom
Row 1: Rep row 1 of Side.

Rows 2–32: Rep row 2 of Side. At end of row 32, fasten off.

Outer Front Pocket
Row 1: Ch 35, sc in 2nd ch from hook, sc in each rem ch across, turn. *(34 sc).*

Rows 2–19: Ch 1; working in **back lps** *(see Stitch Guide)* only, sc in each sc across, turn.

Row 20: Ch 1, sc in each sc across. Fasten off.

Inside Pocket
Row 1: Rep row 1 of Outer Front Pocket.

Rows 2–14: Rep row 2 of Side. At end of row 14, fasten off.

Side Pocket
Row 1: Ch 9, sc in 2nd ch from hook, dc in next ch, [sc in next ch, dc in next ch] across, turn. *(8 sts)*

Rows 2–18: Rep row 2 of Front.

Closing Tab
Row 1: Ch 13, sc in 2nd ch from hook, sc in each rem ch across, turn. *(12 sc)*

Row 2: Ch 1, sc in each sc across, turn.

Row 3: Ch 3 *(counts as first dc through-out)*, dc in each rem sc across, turn.

Row 4: Ch 3, dc in next st, [**fpdc** *(see Stitch Guide)* around post of each of next 2 sts, dc in next st] 3 times, dc in next st, turn. *(12 sts)*

Row 5: Ch 3, dc in next st, [**bpdc** *(see Stitch Guide)* around post of each of next 2 sts, dc in next st] 3 times, dc in next st, turn.

Rows 6–9: Rep rows 4 and 5 alternately.

Row 10: Ch 1, sc in each of next 6 sts, ch 4 for button lp, sc in each of next 6 sts. Fasten off.

Key Chain
Row 1: Ch 6, sc in 2nd ch from hook, sc in each rem ch across, turn. *(5 sc)*
Rows 2–5: Ch 1, sc in each sc across, turn.
Row 6: Ch 1, sc in each of first 3 sc, ch 21, 3 sc in 2nd ch from hook, 3 sc in each rem ch across, sc in each of last 2 sts on last row. Fasten off.

Shoulder Strap
Note: *Make Shoulder Strap only for Purse version.*
Row 1: Ch 7, sc in 2nd ch from hook, sc in each rem ch across, turn. *(6 sc)*
Rows 2–75: Ch 1, sc in first st, [dc in next st, sc in next sc] twice, dc in next st, turn.
Row 76: Ch 1, sc in each st across. Fasten off.
Note: *After purse is assembled, sew Shoulder Strap to each end at top edge of Side pieces.*

Assembly
Note: *If making Wheelchair or Walker Tote, work Assembly before Button Straps.*
With yarn needle, sew Outer Front Pocket to Front piece making sure that Pocket covers only sc rows on Front.
Sew Inside Pocket to inside of Back.
Sew Side Pocket to Side.
Attach the short end of Side Pocket piece, with the pocket opening on top, to the Bottom short end with sc, then attach other end of Bottom to 2nd Side piece with sc.
Sew hook and lp fastening tape to 3rd row from top of 2nd Side piece. Sew opposite side of hook and lp fastening tape centered over rows 1–5 of Key Chain. Attach brass key ring to sc sts at end of curled section of Key Chain.

Holding Pocket Side piece with Pocket opening facing out and opening on top, sc Front and Side pieces tog to bottom, continue to sc around and sc rem Side piece to Front with key ring inside and at top. Rep with Back piece.
Sew Closing Tab to center back top of tote. Sew button centered approximately 2 inches down on Front of Tote.

WHEELCHAIR OR WALKER TOTE
Button Strap
Row 1: Join yarn with sl st to Side piece, ch 1, sc in same st, sc in each of next 3 sts, leave rem 4 sts unworked, turn. *(4 sc)*

Rows 2–14: Ch 1, sc in each sc across, turn. At end of row 14, fasten off.
Sew button to center of row 11 of Button Strap.

Buttonhole Strap
Row 1: Join yarn with sl st in next st of same Side piece as Button Strap, ch 1, sc in same st, sc in each of next 3 sts, turn. *(4 sc)*
Rows 2–14: Ch 1, sc in each sc across, turn.
Row 15: Ch 6, sl st in 4th sc at opposite end of row. Fasten off.
Rep Button Strap and Buttonhole Strap on opposite side. ❏❏

Cozy Shrug

Design by Shirley Zebrowski

SKILL LEVEL

BEGINNER

FINISHED SIZE
31½ x 60 inches

MATERIALS
- ❑ Red Heart Baby Clouds super bulky (super chunky) yarn (6 oz/140 yds/170 g per skein): 6 skeins blue sky #9025 *(A)* **6 SUPER BULKY**
- ❑ Red Heart Super Saver medium (worsted) weight yarn (7 oz/198g /364 yds per skein): 1 skein light blue #381 *(B)* **4 MEDIUM**
- ❑ Sizes I/9/5.5mm and J/10/6mm crochet hooks or sizes needed to obtain gauge
- ❑ Yarn needle

GAUGE
Size J hook and A: 2 shells = 2 inches
Size I hook and B: 7 sc = 2 inches, 7 sc rows = 2 inches

SPECIAL STITCHES
Shell: 5 dc in indicated st.
Single crochet decrease (sc dec): Draw up lp in each of next 3 sts, yo, draw through all 4 lps on hook.

INSTRUCTIONS

SHRUG
Row 1: With size J hook and A, ch 122, sc in 2nd ch from hook, [sk 2 chs, **shell** *(see Special Stitches)* in next ch, sk 2 chs, sc in next ch] across, turn. *(20 shells)*

Row 2: Ch 3 *(counts as first dc throughout)*, 2 dc in same st as beg ch-3, sc in center dc of next shell, [shell in next sc, sc in center dc of next shell] across

to last sc, 3 dc in last sc, turn.

Row 3: Ch 1, sc in first dc, shell in next sc, [sc in center dc of next shell, shell in next sc] across, ending sc in 3rd ch of beg ch-3, turn.

Rows 4–38: Rep rows 2 and 3 alternately, ending with a row 2. At end of row 38, fasten off.

First Cuff

Row 1 (RS): Working in end sts across rows, using size I hook, join B with a sl st over first st at right-hand edge, ch 1; beg in same st and gathering edge slightly, work 49 sc evenly spaced across, turn. *(49 sc)*

Row 2: Ch 1, sc in first sc, [**sc dec** *(see Special Stitches)* in next 3 sc, sc in next sc] across, turn. *(25 sts)*

Rows 3–17: Ch 1; working in **back lps** *(see Stitch Guide)* only, sc in each st across, turn. At end of row 17, do not turn.

Row 18: Ch 1, sc evenly spaced across long edge of Shrug to opposite end. Do not turn. Do not fasten off.

2nd Cuff

Row 1: Ch 1; working in end sts across rows and gathering edge slightly, work 49 sc evenly spaced across, turn. *(49 sc)*

Rows 2–18: Rep rows 2–18 of First Cuff. At end of row 18, fasten off.

Finishing

With yarn needle and B, beg at end of either Cuff, sew seam from beg of Cuff across Shrug for a total of 10 inches. Rep on rem Cuff. ❏❏

Deluxe Lap Robe

Design by Irene Stock

SKILL LEVEL

EASY

FINISHED SIZE

30 inches wide x 40 inches long

MATERIALS

❏ Red Heart Classic medium (worsted) weight yarn (3½ oz/190 yds/99g per skein): 4 skeins each white #1 *(A)* and pale rose #755 *(B)*

4 MEDIUM

❏ Size I/9/5.5mm crochet hook or size needed to obtain gauge
❏ Yarn needle

GAUGE

5 pattern reps = 4 inches; 10 pattern rows = 4 inches

PATTERN NOTE

To change color in last single crochet of row, work last single crochet as follows: insert hook in last stitch, yarn over with working color, draw up a loop, drop working color to wrong side, yaren over with next color, complete single crochet.

INSTRUCTIONS

LAP ROBE

Body

Row 1 (RS): With B, ch 111, dc in 3rd ch from hook, sk 2 chs, *(sc, ch 2, dc) in next ch, sk 2 chs, rep from * across

to last ch, sc in last ch, turn. *(36 dc, 36 sc, 36 ch-2 sps, counting last 2 chs of foundation ch as first ch-2 sp)*

Row 2: (Ch 2, dc) in first sc, (sc, ch 2, dc) in each ch-2 sp across to last ch-2 sp, sc in last ch-2 sp, changing to A, turn.

Rows 3 & 4: With A, rep row 2, changing to B in last sc of row 4.

Rows 5 & 6: With B, rep row 2, changing to A in last sc of row 6.

Rep rows 3–6 alternately until 23 rows of B and 22 rows of A have been worked. At end of last row, fasten off.

Bottom Insert

Row 1: With B, ch 27, rep row 1 of Body. *(8 dc, 8 sc, 8 ch-2 sps, counting last 2 chs of foundation ch as first ch-2 sp)*

Rows 2–6: Rep rows 2–6 of Body.

Rep rows 3-6 alternately until 8 rows of B and 7 rows of A have been worked. At end of last row, fasten off.

Center first row of Bottom Insert to first row of Bottom. Bring remainder of first row around sides of Bottom Insert. Pin in place and sew with yarn needle.

Body Edging

Rnd 1: With WS facing, join white with sl st, ch 1; work in pattern around, join with sl st in beg sc, turn.

Rnd 2: Work in pattern around, join with sl st in beg sc. Fasten off.

Pocket
Make 2.

Rows 1–6: Rep rows 1–6 of Bottom Insert.

Rep rows 3–6 alternately until 5 rows of B and 4 rows of A have been worked. At end of last row, fasten off.

Pocket Edging

Rnds 1 & 2: Rep rnds 1 and 2 for Body Edging.

Tie
Make 2.

With A, ch 101, sl st in 2nd ch from hook, sl st in each rem ch across. Fasten off.

Tie knot in each end.

Fold Tie in half. Pull fold through lp 5 patterns from side and 2 rows from top. Pull ends through lp and pull tight. ❏❏

From simple to sophisticated, home can be many different things in many different places. Whether sprucing up your current dwelling or starting fresh in a new place, these enticing accents will add a personal touch to any domestic setting you call home.

Sunny Tea Cozy

Design by Louise Puchaty

Bless the four corners of this house, its doorway and nooks, its shadows and sun, and those who abide herein, every one.

—*Unknown*

SKILL LEVEL

■□□□
BEGINNER

FINISHED SIZE
Fits 8 x 11 inch teapot

MATERIALS
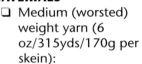
- ❑ Medium (worsted) weight yarn (6 oz/315yds/170g per skein):
    1 skein yellow *(MC)*
    4 yds lime green *(A)*
    3 yds each blue *(B)*, aqua *(C)*, bright orange *(D)* and red orange *(E)*
- ❑ Medium (worsted) weight yarn (3 oz/165 yds/85g per skein):
    3 yds each ruby red *(F)* and purple *(G)*
- ❑ Sizes F/5/3.75mm, G/6/4mm and K/10½/6.5mm crochet hooks or sizes needed to obtain gauge
- ❑ Yarn needle

GAUGE
Size F hook: Leaf = ¾ inch
Size G hook: Flower = 1½ inches
Size K hook and 2 strands held tog: 6 sc = 2 inches, 6 rows sc = 2 inches

INSTRUCTIONS
COZY
Front
Row 1 (WS): With size K hook, holding 2 strands MC tog, ch 32, sc in 2nd ch from hook, sc in each rem ch across, turn. *(31 sc)*
Row 2: Ch 1, sc in first sc, [sc in **front lp** *(see Stitch Guide)* only of next sc, sc in next sc] across, turn.
Row 3: Ch 1, sc in first sc, [sc in **back**

lp *(see Stitch Guide)* only of next sc, sc in next sc] across, turn.

Rows 4–20: Rep rows 2 and 3 alternately, ending with a row 2.

Row 21: Ch 1, sc in first sc, [**sc dec** *(see Stitch Guide)* in back lps only of next 2 sc, sc in next sc] across, turn. *(21 sts)*

Row 22: Ch 1, sc in first st, [sc in back lp only of next st, sc in next st] across, turn.

Row 23: Rep row 3.

Row 24: Ch 1, sc in first sc, [sc dec in front lps only of next 2 sc, sc dec in back lps only of next 2 sc] across, turn. *(11 sts)*

Row 25: Ch 1, sc in first st, [sc in back lp only of next st, sc in next sc] across. Fasten off.

Back
Rows 1–25: Rep rows 1–25 of Front.

Flower
Make 1 each B, C, D, E, F and G.
With size G hook, ch 7, join with sl st to form ring, sl st in ring, [ch 1, dc, tr, dc, sl st] 5 times in ring. Fasten off.

Leaf
Make 6.
With size F hook and A, ch 13, sl st in 13th ch from hook. Fasten off.

Assembly
Using photo as a guide, sew Flowers and Leaves to Front of Cozy.

Holding Front and Back of Cozy with WS tog, beg at bottom, sew up 2 inches on each side. Beg at top, sew down 2 inches of each side, leaving rem of sides open for tea spout and teapot handle. ❏❏

Basket-Weave Pot Holder & Hot Pad

Designs by Dot Drake

SKILL LEVEL

EASY

FINISHED SIZE
7 inches square

MATERIALS
☐ Medium (worsted) weight yarn:
  1¾ oz/88 yds/50g each pink, yellow and green
☐ Size G/6/4mm crochet hook or size needed to obtain gauge
☐ Yarn needle
☐ Straight pins

GAUGE
4 sc = 1 inch

INSTRUCTIONS

POT HOLDER
Strip
Make 8 each yellow and pink.
Row 1: Ch 25, sc in 2nd ch from hook, sc in each rem ch across, turn. *(24 sc)*
Row 2: Ch 1, sc in each sc across. Fasten off.

Assembly
On a flat surface, working outward from center, weave Strips in basket-weave style, positioning Strips so that no spaces show between Strips. Pin Strips tog.

Border
Rnd 1 (RS): Attach green in any Strip on outer edge, removing straight pins as work progresses, ch 1, sc evenly sp around, working 3 sc in each corner, join with sl st in beg sc, turn.
Rnd 2: Ch 1, sc in same sc as joining, tr in next sc, [sc in next sc, tr in next sc] around, working (sc, ch 8, sc) in any corner sc for hanging loop; join with sl st in beg sc. Fasten off.

HOT PAD
Strip
Make 8 each yellow and green.
Rows 1 & 2: Rep rows 1 and 2 of Pot Holder.

Assembly
Rep Assembly for Pot Holder.

Border
Rnd 1: With pink, rep rnd 1 of Pot Holder Border.
Rnd 2: Ch 2, sc in same sc as joining, tr in next sc, [sc in next sc, tr in next sc] around, join with sl st in beg sc. Fasten off. ☐☐

Happy is the house that shelters a friend.

—*Ralph Waldo Emerson*

Scrubbie Dishcloths

Designs by Norma Gale

GREEN DISHCLOTH
FINISHED SIZE
11 inches square

MATERIALS
- ❏ Crochet cotton size 10:
  325 yds mint green *(A)*
- ❏ Nylon thread:
  125 yds teal blue *(B)*
- ❏ Size 7/1.65mm steel crochet hook or size needed to obtain gauge

GAUGE
21 dc = 2 inches; 8 rows in pattern st = 1 inch

INSTRUCTIONS
DISHCLOTH
Row 1: With A, ch117, dc in 4th ch from hook, dc in each rem ch across, turn. *(115 dc, counting last 3 chs of foundation ch as first dc)*

Row 2: Ch 3 *(counts as first dc throughout)*, dc in each of next 2 dc, dc in **back lp** *(see Stitch Guide)* only of next dc, [dc in next dc, dc in back lp only of next dc] across to last 3 dc, dc in each of last 3 dc. Do not turn. Drop A. Do not fasten off.

Row 3: Join B with sl st in first rem lp on row before last, ch 4 *(counts as first dc, ch-1)*, dc in next rem lp, [ch 1, dc in next rem lp] across. Fasten off. Turn. *(55 dc, 54 ch-1 sps)*

Row 4: With dropped A, draw up lp in first dc on row before last, ch 3, dc in each of next 2 dc on row before last, dc in next st on row before last and on last row at the same time, [dc in next st on row before last, dc in next st on row before last and last row at the same time] across to last 3 sts on row before last, dc in each of last 3 sts, turn. *(115 dc)*

Rows 5–85: Rep rows 2–4 consecutively. At end of row 85, do not fasten off.

Edging
Rnd 1: Ch 1, sc in each st around, working 2 sc over end st of each row across sides and 3 sc in each corner st, join with sl st in beg sc.

Rnd 2: Sl st in each st around, join with sl st in beg sl st. Fasten off.

PINK DISHCLOTH
FINISHED SIZE
11 inches square

MATERIALS
- ❏ Crochet cotton size 10:
  225 yd white *(A)*, 100 yds variegated *(B)*
- ❏ Nylon thread:
  80 yds hot pink *(C)*
- ❏ Size 7/1.65mm steel crochet hook or size needed to obtain gauge

GAUGE
21 sc = 2 inches; 14 rows in pattern stitch = 1 inch

INSTRUCTIONS
DISHCLOTH
Row 1: With A, ch 109, sc in 2nd ch from hook, sc in each rem ch across, turn. *(108 sc)*

Rows 2 & 3: Ch 1, sc in each sc across,

turn. At end of last row, drop white.

Row 4: Working in **back lps** (see Stitch Guide) only, join C with sl st in 3rd sc, dc in same sc, sl st in next sc, [dc in next sc, sl st in next sc] across to last 2 sc, leave last 2 sc unworked. Fasten off. Do not turn.

Row 5 (WS): Pick up dropped lp of A, ch 1, sc in each of first 2 sts of row before last, sk joining sl st on last row, [sc in **front lp** (see Stitch Guide) only of next st on row before last and back lp only of next st on last row at the same time] across to last 2 sts on row before last, sc in each of last 2 sts, drop A. Turn.

Row 6: Join B with a sl st in first sc, ch 1, sc in same sc, sc in next sc, [ch 1, sk next sc, sc in next sc] across to last 2 sc, sc in each of last 2 sc, turn. (56 sc, 52 ch-1 sps)

Row 7: Ch 1, sc in each of first 2 sc, [ch 1, sc in next sp] across to last 2 sc, sc in each of last 2 sc, drop B. Turn.

Row 8: Pick up dropped A, ch 1, sc in each sc and each sp across. Drop white. Turn. (108 sc)

Rows 9–133: Rep rows 4–8 consecutively. At end of row 133, fasten off B.

Rows 134 & 135: Rep rows 4 and 5. At end of row 135, fasten off C.

Rows 136 & 137: With A, ch 1, sc in each st across, turn. At end of row 137, fasten off.

Edging

Rnd 1: Join B with a sl st in first sc on last row, ch 1, sc in same sc, 2 sc in next sc, sc in each sc across to last sc, 3 sc in last sc; *evenly space 107 sc across ends of rows*; working in rem lps of foundation ch at base of row 1, 3 sc in first st, 2 sc in next st, sc in each st across to last st, 3 sc in last st, rep from * to *, join with sl st in beg sc. (109 sc across each side between corner sc)

Rnd 2: Ch 1, 2 sc in same sc as joining, *[ch 1, sk next sc, {sc in next sc, ch 1, sk next sc} across] to next corner sc, 3 sc in corner sc, rep from * twice, rep between [ ], sc in same sc as beg sc, join with sl st in beg sc.

Rnd 3: Ch 1, 2 sc in first sc, *[ch 1, sk next st, {sc in next sp, ch 1, sk next st} across] to corner sc, 3 sc in corner sc, rep from * twice, rep between [ ], sc in same sc as beg sc, join with sl st in beg sc. Fasten off.

Rnd 4: Join A with sl st in first sc, ch 1, 2 sc in same sc, sc in each st and sp around, working 3 sc in each corner sc, sc in same sc as beg sc, join with sl st in beg sc.

Rnd 5: Sl st in each sc around, join with sl st in beg sl st. Fasten off.

SCRAP DISHCLOTH

FINISHED SIZE
11 inches square

MATERIALS
- ❏ Crochet cotton size 10: 140 yds white, 40 yds each pink and yellow 35 yds each green, peach and purple
- ❏ Nylon thread: 125 yds teal blue
- ❏ Size 7/1.65mm steel crochet hook or size needed to obtain gauge

GAUGE
21 dc = 2 inches; 8 rows in pattern stitch = 1 inch

INSTRUCTIONS

DISHCLOTH

Rows 1 & 2: With white, rep rows 1 and 2 of Green Dishcloth. At end of row 2, do not turn. Fasten off.

Row 3: With teal, rep row 3 of Green Dishcloth.

Row 4: Join pink with sl st in first st on row before last, ch 3, dc in each of next 2 dc on row before last, dc in next st on row before last and on last row at the same time, [dc in next st on row before last, dc in next st on row before last and last row at the same time] across to last 3 sts on row before last, dc in each of last 3 sts. Fasten off. Turn. (115 dc)

Row 5: Join yellow with sl st in first st, rep row 2. Do not turn. Fasten off.

Row 6: Rep row 3.

Rows 7–82: Working in color sequence of white, teal, green, teal, peach, teal, white, teal, purple, teal, white, teal, pink, teal, yellow and teal, rep rows 4–6 consecutively, ending with a row 4.

Row 83: With white, rep row 5.

Row 84: Rep row 6.

Row 85: With white, rep row 4. Do not fasten off.

Edging

Rnd 1: Ch 1, sc in each st and 2 sc over end st of each row around, working 3 sc in each corner, join with sl st in beg sc.

Rnd 2: Sl st in each sc around, join with sl st in beg sl st. Fasten off. ❏❏

A thoughtful, handmade gift is the very best kind of present and creates a warm and lasting memory for the recipient. Whether celebrating a birthday, housewarming or other special occasion, a gift made by hand and given from the heart is always appreciated.

Floral Bouquet

Design by Stephanie Coleman

SKILL LEVEL

BEGINNER

FINISHED SIZE

2¾ inches across widest point

MATERIALS

- ❏ Crochet cotton size 10:
     10 yds each green, red, pink and white
- ❏ Size 7/1.65 steel crochet hook or size needed to obtain gauge
- ❏ Tapestry needle
- ❏ 3 iridescent 5mm sequins
- ❏ 1-inch pin back
- ❏ Craft glue

GAUGE

Flower = 1 inch in diameter

SPECIAL STITCH

Picot: Ch 3, sl st in 3rd ch from hook.

INSTRUCTIONS

FLOWER

Make 1 each white, red and pink.

Rnd 1: Ch 2, (sc, ch 3) 5 times in 2nd ch from hook, join with sl st in beg sc. *(5 ch-3 sps)*

Rnd 2: (Sl st, ch 1, 4 dc, ch 1, sl st) in each ch-3 sp around, join with sl st in beg sl st. Fasten off.

Glue 1 sequin to center of each Flower.

BASE & LEAVES

Base

Rnd 1: With green, ch 4, 11 dc in 4th ch from hook, join with sl st in 4th ch of beg ch-4. *(12 dc, counting last 3 chs of beg ch-4 as first dc)*

Rnd 2: Ch 2 *(counts as first hdc throughout)*, hdc in same dc as joining, 2 hdc in each dc around, join with sl st in 2nd ch of beg ch-2. *(24 hdc)*

Rnd 3: Ch 1, sc in same hdc as joining, ch 6, sc in each of next 3 hdc, ch 6, sc in each of last 20 hdc, join with sl st in beg sc. Do not fasten off. *(2 ch-6 sps)*

Leaves

Row 1: *(Sl st, ch 3, 5 dc, **picot**—*see Special Stitch*, 6 dc) in ch-6 sp*, sc in each of next 3 sc, rep between *, sl st in next sc, leave rem sts unworked, Fasten off.

Using photo as a guide, glue Flowers to front of Base.

Glue pin back to back of Base. ❏❏

No act of kindness, no matter how small, is ever wasted.

—*Aesop*

Gardener's Bookmark

Design by Katherine Eng

SKILL LEVEL

EASY

FINISHED SIZE

8½ inches long without ribbon

MATERIALS

- ❑ Crochet cotton size 10:
    15 yds white
    8 yds each pink and green
    5 yds yellow
- ❑ Size 5/1.90mm steel crochet hook or size needed to obtain gauge
- ❑ 8-inches length ⅛-inch-wide ribbon

GAUGE

Flower = 2 inches across widest point

SPECIAL STITCHES

Bobble: Holding back last lp of each st on hook, 2 tr 3rd, 4th and 5th heads in indicated st, yo, draw through all 3 lps on hook.

Joining chain-2 (joining ch-2): Ch 1, remove hook from lp, insert hook in indicated st, pick up dropped lp, draw through st, ch 1.

INSTRUCTIONS

BOOKMARK

First Flower

Rnd 1: With white, ch 3, join with sl st to form ring, ch 1, 12 sc in ring, join with sl st in beg sc. Fasten off. *(12 sc)*

Rnd 2: Join pink with sl st in any sc, (ch 4, **bobble**—*see Special Stitches,* ch 4, sl st) in same sc as joining, ch 2, sk next sc, [(sl st, ch 4, bobble, ch 4, sl st) in next st, ch 2, sk next st] around, join with sl st in same st as beg sl st. Fasten off.

Rnd 3: Join white with sl st in any ch-2 sp, ch 1, sc in same sp, ch 4, (sc, ch 2, sc) in top of next bobble, ch 4, *sc in next ch-2 sp, ch 4, (sc, ch 2, sc) in top of next bobble, ch 4, rep from * around, join with sl st in beg sc. Fasten off.

2nd Flower

Rnd 1: Rep rnd 1 of First Flower.

Rnd 2: With green, rep rnd 2 of First Flower.

Rnd 3: Join white with sl st in any ch-2 sp, ch 1, sc in same sp, ch 4, (sc, **joining ch-2**—*see Special Stitches*—to corresponding ch-2 sp at top of any bobble on previous Flower, sc) in top of next bobble on working Flower, ch 4, sc in next ch-2 sp, ch 4, (sc, joining ch-2 to ch-2 sp at top of next bobble on previous Flower, sc) in top of next bobble on working Flower, ch 4, sc in next ch-2 sp, continue around as for rnd 3 of First Flower.

3rd Flower

Rnd 1: Rep rnd 1 of First Flower.

Rnd 2: With yellow, rep rnd 2 of First Flower.

Rnd 3: Rep rnd 3 of 2nd Flower, working joinings directly across from 2 joinings of previous 2 Flowers.

4th Flower

Rnds 1–3: Rep rnds 1–3 of 2nd Flower.

5th Flower

Rnds 1 & 2: Rep rnds 1 and 2 of First Flower.

Rnd 3: Rep rnd 3 of 2nd Flower.

Finishing

Fold ribbon in half. Insert fold in ch-2 sp at bottom of 5th Flower and pull ends through to form loop. Pull loose ends through loop. Pull to tighten. ❑❑

Mini Purselette

Design by Eleanor Miles-Bradley

SKILL LEVEL

BEGINNER

FINISHED SIZE

2¼ x 2¼ inches excluding fringe

MATERIALS

- ❑ Pearl cotton size 5 crochet cotton: 50 yds variegated pastels
- ❑ Size 0/2.50mm steel crochet hook or size needed to obtain gauge
- ❑ 2 gold rings each 1-inch in diameter

GAUGE

7 sc = 1 inch; 4 sc rows = ½ inch

PATTERN NOTE

Weave in loose ends as work progresses.

INSTRUCTIONS

PURSE
Make 2.

Row 1: Join crochet cotton over ring with sl st, ch 1, 15 sc over ring, turn. *(15 sc)*

Rows 2–13: Ch 1, sc in each sc across, turn. At end of row 13, fasten off.

Assembly

Holding both Purse pieces tog and working through both thicknesses at once, join crochet cotton with sl st over end st of row 1, ch 1, sc in same st as joining, sc evenly sp around 3 sides of Purse to opposite side of row 1, working 2 sc in each corner, sl st in same st as last sc, ch 150 for neck strap, sl st in first sc at opposite side of row 1. Fasten off.

Fringe

Cut 30 4-inch lengths of crochet cotton. Working across 15 sc of Purse bottom, [fold 2 strands held tog in half, insert hook in sc, draw folded end through to form lp, draw cut ends through lp on hook, pull ends lightly to secure] across Bottom. Trim ends evenly. ❑❑

May no gift be too small to give,
nor too simple to receive, which is wrapped
in thoughtfulness and tied with love.

—*L.O. Baird*

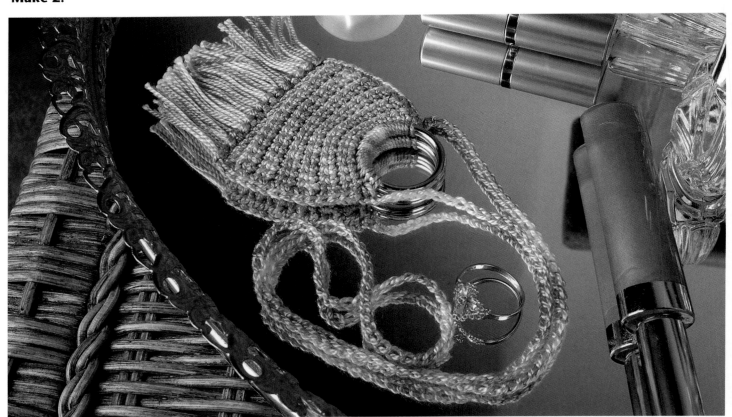

Lovely Bible Cover

Design by Louise Puchaty

SKILL LEVEL

EASY

FINISHED SIZE
4½ inches x 6½ inches

MATERIALS
- ❑ Crochet cotton size 20:
    400 yds ecru, 20 yds white
- ❑ Size 10/1.15mm steel crochet hook or size needed to obtain gauge
- ❑ Tapestry needle
- ❑ Sewing needle
- ❑ Sewing thread
- ❑ 7½ x 16½ inch blue satin fabric
- ❑ 3½ inches ¼-inch-wide blue ribbon
- ❑ Fabric stiffener
- ❑ Plastic wrap
- ❑ Pinning board
- ❑ Straight pins
- ❑ Fabric glue
- ❑ 1¾-inch piece of cardboard

GAUGE
({3 dc, ch 3} 4 times, 3 dc) = 2 inches

SPECIAL STITCHES
Shell: (3 dc, ch 2, 3 dc) in indicated st or sp.

Picot: Ch 3, sl st in last sc made.

INSTRUCTIONS
COVER
Outer Panel
Row 1: With ecru, ch 138, dc in 6th ch from hook, dc in each of next 2 chs, ch 3, dc in next ch, *sk next 2 chs, dc in each of next 3 chs, ch 3, dc in next ch, rep from * across to last 3 chs, dc in last ch, turn. *(90 dc, counting last 3 chs of foundation ch as first dc)*

Row 2: Ch 3 *(counts as first dc throughout)*, (3 dc, ch 3, dc) in each ch-3 sp across, dc in last ch of foundation ch, turn.

Row 3: Ch 3, (3 dc, ch 3, dc) in each ch-3 sp across, dc in 3rd ch of beg ch-3, turn.

Rows 4–32: Rep row 3. At end of row 32, do not fasten off. Turn.

Edging
Ch 3, **shell** *(see Special Stitches)* in each ch-3 sp across; *working over ends of rows, shell over end st of every other row across*; working across ch sps of foundation row at base of row 1, shell in each sp across; rep from * to *, join with sl st in 3rd ch of beg ch-3. Fasten off.

First Inner Panel
Row 1: With ecru, ch 42, rep row 1 of Outer Panel. *(26 dc, counting last 3 chs of foundation ch as first dc)*

Rows 2–32: Rep rows 2–32 of Outer Panel. At end of row 32, do not fasten off. Do not turn.

First Inner Panel Edging
Ch 3; working over ends of rows across long edge, shell over end st of every other row across to bottom, dc in bottom corner. Fasten off.

2nd Inner Panel

Rows 1–32: Rep rows 1–32 of First Inner Panel. At end of row 32, fasten off. Do not turn.

2nd Inner Panel Edging

Join yarn with a sl st in opposite bottom corner, ch 3; working over ends of rows across long edge, shell over end st of every other row across to top, dc in top corner. Fasten off.

Assembly

With yarn and tapestry needle, sew 3 edges without Edging on First Inner Panel to corresponding 3 edges of Outer Panel. Sew 3 edges without Edging on 2nd Inner Panel to rem 3 corresponding edges of Outer Panel.

Cross
Make 2.

With white, ch 12, join with sl st to form ring, ch 18, sl st in 12th ch from hook, ch 6, sk next 5 unworked chs of ch-18, sl st in next ch; working around first ch-12 ring, ({3 sc, ch 12, sl st in last sc made} 3 times, 3 sc) in ch-12 ring; (3 sc, **picot**—see Special Stitches, 3 sc) in next ch-6 sp; * (3 sc, {picot, 3 sc} 3 times) in ch-12 ring*, (3 sc, picot, 3 sc) in ch-6 sp; ** sl st in each of next 3 sc, bet *, rep from ** twice, sl st in each of last 3 sts. Fasten off.

Saturate Crosses with fabric stiffener, pin to plastic wrap-covered pinning board. Let dry completely. Cut blue ribbon to size and glue to back on 1 Cross. Set aside rem Cross for Bookmark.

Center ribbon-trimmed Cross to front of Outer Panel 1¾ inches down from top edge. With sewing needle and sewing thread, sew in place.

Lining

Sew a ¼-inch seam all around blue satin fabric. With WS facing, turn up each short side 2½ inches and sew top and bottom in place to Lining with sewing needle and sewing thread. Place over Bible. Place Bible Cover over Lining.

BOOKMARK

Join ecru with a sl st to center bottom picot of rem Cross, ch 90, sc in 2nd ch from hook, sc in each rem ch across. Fasten off. Dampen sc row and pin flat to dry.

Tassel

Cut 2 lengths of ecru each 4 inches long and set aside. Wrap ecru around cardboard piece 20 times. Tie one 4-inch length around bundle at top of Tassel. Cut threads at opposite end. Tie rem 4-inch length ⅛ inch from top of Tassel. Sew Tassel to Bookmark. ❏❏

Accessory Pockets

Designs by Sharon Phillips

SKILL LEVEL

BEGINNER

FINISHED SIZE

Cell Phone Case: 3 x 6 inches
Eyewear Case: 3½ x 7½ inches

MATERIALS

☐ J & P Coats Luster Sheen fine (sport) weight yarn (4 oz/335 yds/ 113g per skein):
  1 skein spa blue #821
☐ Size F/5/3.75mm crochet hook or size needed to obtain gauge
☐ Sewing needle and matching sewing thread
☐ 2 decorative ¾-inch flower buttons

2 FINE

GAUGE

6 dc = 1 inch; 4 pattern rnds = 1 inch

SPECIAL STITCHES

Shell: 3 dc in indicated st.
Beginning shell (beg shell): (Ch 3, 2 dc) in indicated st.

INSTRUCTIONS
CELL PHONE CASE

Rnd 1: Ch 14, 6 dc in 4th ch from hook, dc in each of next 9 chs, 7 dc in last ch; working in rem lps across opposite side of foundation ch, dc in each of next 9 chs, join with sl st in last ch of foundation ch. *(32 dc, counting last 3 chs of foundation ch as first dc)*

Rnd 2: Ch 1, sc in same st as joining, *sk next dc, **shell** (see Special Stitches) in next dc, sk next dc**, sc in next dc, rep from * around, ending last rep at **, join with sl st in beg sc. *(8 shells)*

Rnd 3: Beg shell (see Special Stitches) in same sc as joining, sc in center dc of next shell, [shell in next sc, sc in center dc of next shell] around, join with sl st in 3rd ch of beg ch-3.

Rnd 4: Sl st in next dc, ch 1, sc in same dc, shell in next sc, [sc in center dc of next shell, shell in next sc] around, join with sl st in beg sc.

Rnds 5–19: Rep rnds 3 and 4 alternately, ending with a rnd 3. At end of rnd 19, turn.

Strap

Row 1: (Sl st, ch 3—*counts as first dc*, dc) in next sc, sc in center dc of next shell, shell in next sc, sc in center dc of next shell, 2 dc in next sc, leave rem sts unworked, turn. *(7 dc, 2 sc)*

Row 2: Ch 1, sc in first dc, shell in next sc, sc in center dc of next shell, shell in next sc, sc in 3rd ch of beg ch-3, turn. *(2 shells, 3 sc)*

Row 3: Ch 3, dc in first sc, sc in center dc of next shell, shell in next sc, sc in center dc of next shell, 2 dc in last sc, turn.

Rows 4–9: Rep rows 2 and 3 alternately.

Row 10: Ch 1, sc in first dc, 2 dc in next sc, sc in center dc of next shell, 2 dc in next sc, sc in 3rd ch of beg ch-3, turn. *(3 sc, 4 dc)*

Row 11: Ch 1, sc in first sc, (2 dc, ch 5, 2 dc) in next sc for button lp, sc in last sc. Fasten off.

Strap Edging

With RS facing, join yarn with sl st over end st of row 1 of strap, ch 1, sc in same st; working over end sts of rows across Strap, work 2 sc over each dc end st and 1 sc over each sc end st to ch 5 sp, 5 sc in ch-5 sp, continue in established pattern to end st of row 1 on opposite side of Strap. Fasten off.

With sewing needle and sewing thread, sew button to center front of Case over rnd 14.

EYEWEAR CASE

Rnd 1: Ch 5, join to form a ring, ch 3 *(counts as first dc throughout)*, 19 dc in ring, join with sl st in 3rd ch of beg ch-3. *(20 dc)*

Rnd 2: (Ch 3, dc) in same dc as joining, 2 dc in each rem dc around, join with sl st in 3rd ch of beg ch-3. *(40 dc)*

Rnd 3: Rep rnd 2 of Cell Phone Case. *(10 shells)*

Rnds 4–26: Rep rnds 3 and 4 of Cell Phone Case alternately, ending with a rnd 3. At end of rnd 26, turn.

Strap

Rows 1–11: Rep rows 1–11 of Strap for Cell Phone Case.

Strap Edging

Rep instructions for Strap Edging for Cell Phone Case.

With sewing needle and sewing thread, sew button to center front of Case over rnd 20. ❑❑

HATS FOR THE HOMELESS

Hats for the Homeless was created in memory of John Carroll, a young man who would annually gather his friends during the holiday season and, together with them, roam the streets of New York giving warm hats, scarves and gloves to the homeless. After John's sudden death in 1998, it became the mission of Hats for the Homeless to continue his tradition of bringing warmth and comfort to the less fortunate.

Through Hats for the Homeless, hats, scarves and gloves are collected throughout the year, gift-wrapped and distributed to a large population of urban homeless. The organization welcomes donations from anyone who would like to crochet, knit or purchase a new hat, scarf or pair of gloves to send them.

Wrapping donated gifts would be very helpful. For more information on Hats for the Homeless, visit their Web site at www.hats4thehomeless.org, e-mail them at info@hats4thehomeless.org, or write to Hats for the Homeless, 905 Main St., Hackensack, NJ 07601.

HUGS FOR HOMELESS ANIMALS

Hugs for Homeless Animals (H4HA) is a multiservice, nonprofit organization dedicated to helping homeless and

displaced animals worldwide. Their popular Snuggles Project was established by H4HA president and founder Rae French in 1996 to provide security blankets, called "Snuggles," to shelter animals as a comforting reprieve from their hard, cold surroundings and to help them feel less alone.

The Snuggles Project asks for donations of handmade blankets to local humane societies and animal shelters. The blankets can be crocheted, knitted or sewn in the following guideline sizes: 14 x 14 inches (small), 24 x 24 inches (medium) and 36 x 36 inches (large). They may be cotton or acrylic in any color and should not have fringe that animals can chew off and swallow. Yarn or thread ends should be double-knotted and securely woven into the fabric. Snuggles are great projects for kids or people learning how to crochet, knit or sew because the blankets don't have to be perfect. The animals love them any way they can get them!

For more information about the Hugs for Homeless Animals organization, plus free crochet, knitting and sewing patterns to make Snuggles blankets, visit their Web site at www.h4ha.org.

NEWBORNS IN NEED

Newborns in Need is a charity devoted to providing essentials for sick and needy premature and newborn infants whose mothers literally have nothing. Babies are going home from the hospital in nothing more than a disposable diaper, and sometimes "home" is a shelter for battered women or the homeless.

Founded in 1992 by Carol and Richard Green of Houston, Mo., Newborns in Need provides over 21,000 much-needed preemie and newborn items each month to individuals, medical centers, hospitals, homeless shelters, adoption agencies, sheriff's offices and food pantries throughout the United States.

NIN gratefully accepts crocheted, knitted and sewn blankets, clothing, accessories, toys and other needs such as burial layettes, as well as donations of yarn, crochet cotton, fabric, flannelette, stuffing, batting, ribbon and sewing notions for NIN's 11,000 volunteers to use in making these items.

To find out how to help or get information on starting a local NIN group, visit their Web site at www.newbornsinneed.org, e-mail them at office@newbornsinneed.org, or contact Newborns in Need, P.O. Box 385, 112 West Main Street, Houston, MO 65483, (417) 967-9441.

PROJECT LINUS

Project Linus is a 100 percent volunteer, nonprofit organization dedicated to providing love, warmth and comfort to children who are seriously ill, traumatized or otherwise in need through the gifts of new, handmade, washable blankets and afghans lovingly created by volunteer "blanketeers."

Founded in 1995 by Karen Loucks-Baker of Parker, Colo., and named after the blanket-carrying character in the *Peanuts* comic strip, Project Linus now has over 300 chapters in the United States and has delivered over half a million security blankets to children around the world. The project has been featured in leading magazines and on the Rosie O'Donnell and Oprah Winfrey shows.

For more information and a listing of national chapters, visit their Web site as www.projectlinus.org, which also has links to numerous free patterns to make crocheted, knitted or quilted blankets. You may also contact them at Project Linus National Headquarters, P.O. Box 5621, Bloomington, IL 61702-5621, (309) 664-7814.

WARMING FAMILIES

As a project of the One Heart Foundation, Warming Families is an all-volunteer service that delivers blankets, clothing and other warm items to the homeless, domestic violence shelters and nursing homes.

Warming Families receives no financial funding, and all donations of time and materials are given directly to helping needy recipients. Donated items may be purchased or handmade. The Warming Families Web site offers many free crochet, knitting and craft patterns to make afghans, blankets, toys, dolls and all types of warm clothing and accessories for all ages from infants to seniors.

For more information, visit their Web site at www.warmingfamilies.org, e-mail project co-founder Suzanne Osmond at suzanne@oneheart.org, or write One Heart Foundation, P.O. Box 400, Orem, UT 84057.

WARM UP AMERICA!

Warm Up America! is a project sponsored by the Craft Yarn Council of America that is dedicated to keeping people-in-need warm with handmade afghans and blankets. They ask for volunteers, working together with family, friends or groups, to crochet or knit 7 x 9-inch sections, assemble them into afghans and distribute them to needy recipients in their own communities.

When this is not possible, the Council will gladly accept donations of individual sections or strips needing assembly, or completed afghans. They also welcome entire afghans that are crocheted or knitted in any colors from any patterns. The Council distributes completed blankets to social service agencies who have contacted their office.

For more information on the Warm Up America! project, plus free crochet and knitting patterns for making afghan sections, afghan assembly tips, and basic crochet and knitting instructions, visit their Web site at www.craftyarncouncil.com/warmup.html. Donated items should be sent to Warm Up America!, 2500 Lowell Road, Gastonia, NC 28054. ❏❏

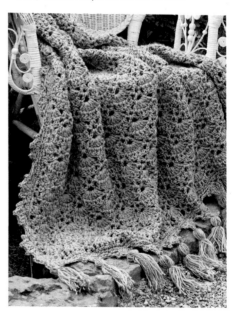

306 East Parr Road
Berne, IN 46711
© 2006 Annie's Attic

TOLL-FREE ORDER LINE or to request a free catalog (800) LV-ANNIE (800) 582-6643
Customer Service (800) AT-ANNIE (800) 282-6643, **Fax** (800) 882-6643
Visit www.AnniesAttic.com

ISBN-10: 1-59635-090-3   ISBN-13: 978-1-59635-090-8

Printed in USA   1 2 3 4 5 6 7 8 9

Stitch Guide

ABBREVIATIONS

beg	begin/beginning
bpdc	back post double crochet
bpsc	back post single crochet
bptr	back post treble crochet
CC	contrasting color
ch	chain stitch
ch-	refers to chain or space previously made (i.e., ch-1 space)
ch sp	chain space
cl	cluster
cm	centimeter(s)
dc	double crochet
dec	decrease/decreases/decreasing
dtr	double treble crochet
fpdc	front post double crochet
fpsc	front post single crochet
fptr	front post treble crochet
g	gram(s)
hdc	half double crochet
inc	increase/increases/increasing
lp(s)	loop(s)
MC	main color
mm	millimeter(s)
oz	ounce(s)
pc	popcorn
rem	remain/remaining
rep	repeat(s)
rnd(s)	round(s)
RS	right side
sc	single crochet
sk	skip(ped)
sl st	slip stitch
sp(s)	space(s)
st(s)	stitch(es)
tog	together
tr	treble crochet
trtr	triple treble
WS	wrong side
yd(s)	yard(s)
yo	yarn over

Chain—ch: Yo, pull through lp on hook.

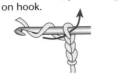

Slip stitch—sl st: Insert hook in st, yo, pull through both lps on hook.

Single crochet—sc: Insert hook in st, yo, pull through st, yo, pull through both lps on hook.

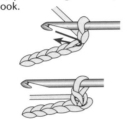

Front loop—front lp
Back loop—back lp

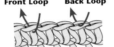

Front post stitch—fp:
Back post stitch—bp: When working post st, insert hook from right to left around post st on previous row.

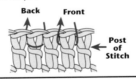

Half double crochet—hdc: Yo, insert hook in st, yo, pull through st, yo, pull through all 3 lps on hook.

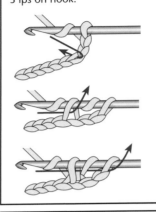

Double crochet—dc: Yo, insert hook in st, yo, pull through st, [yo, pull through 2 lps] twice.

Change colors: Drop first color; with 2nd color, pull through last 2 lps of st.

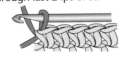

Treble crochet—tr: Yo 2 times, insert hook in st, yo, pull through st, [yo, pull through 2 lps] 3 times.

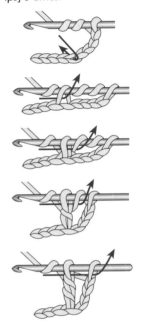

Double treble crochet—dtr: Yo 3 times, insert hook in st, yo, pull through st, [yo, pull through 2 lps] 4 times.

Single crochet decrease (sc dec): (Insert hook, yo, draw up a lp) in each of the sts indicated, yo, draw through all lps on hook.

Example of 2-sc dec

Half double crochet decrease (hdc dec): (Yo, insert hook, yo, draw lp through) in each of the sts indicated, yo, draw through all lps on hook.

Example of 2-hdc dec

Double crochet decrease (dc dec): (Yo, insert hook, yo, draw lp through, yo, draw through 2 lps on hook) in each of the sts indicated, yo, draw through all lps on hook.

Example of 2-dc dec

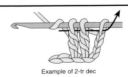

Example of 2-tr dec

Treble crochet decrease (tr dec): Holding back last lp of each st, tr in each of the sts indicated, yo, pull through all lps on hook.

US		UK
sl st (slip stitch)	=	sc (single crochet)
sc (single crochet)	=	dc (double crochet)
hdc (half double crochet)	=	htr (half treble crochet)
dc (double crochet)	=	tr (treble crochet)
tr (treble crochet)	=	dtr (double treble crochet)
dtr (double treble crochet)	=	ttr (triple treble crochet)
skip	=	miss

For more complete information, visit
AnniesAttic.com